SOMERSET VOICES
A Celebration of Memories

SOMERSET VOICES
A Celebration of Memories

ANN HEELEY, LOUISE CLAPP, LIZ SNELGROVE

Friends of the Somerset Rural Life Museum

First published in Great Britain in 2010

The transcriptions and the recordings are available by appointment at The Somerset Rural Life Museum, Glastonbury.
Times of opening Tuesday – Saturday 10.am – 5.00pm
Contact: 01458 831197

Photograph on page 2: *Thatching a rick near Chard in 1950.*
Photograph on page 3: *Taking sheep to the Michaelmas Fair at Bridgwater, which was held on the*
Wednesday after Michaelmas day and the two days following.

British Library Cataloguing-in-Publication Data
A CIP record for this title is available from the British Library

ISBN 978 0 86183 447 1

SOMERSET BOOKS
Somerset Books is a partnership between DAA Halsgrove and
Somerset County Council (Directorate of Culture and Heritage)
www.somerset.gov.uk
Halsgrove House,
Ryelands Industrial Estate,
Bagley Road, Wellington, Somerset TA21 9PZ
Tel: 01823 653777   Fax: 01823 216796
email: sales@halsgrove.com

Part of the Halsgrove group of companies
Information on all Halsgrove titles is available at: www.halsgrove.com

Printed and bound by Grafiche Flaminia, Italy

CONTENTS

A fisherman striding across the shore of the Bristol Channel towards the salmon fishing butts in 1977.

FOREWORD

THERE IS NOTHING LIKE the human voice! Historians of past generations depended almost entirely on the written word, usually what someone else wrote long after the event. They became excited when they found eye-witness accounts that added at least some sort of authenticity, but somehow the style was formal, the work of an onlooker rather than a participant. Diaries and autobiography were often a careful selection of activities, memories and opinions of people of social or political status who thought that the records of their lives were worth sharing. But most ordinary people were too busy for that sort of thing and would not have believed that anyone would care to know how they lived and what they hoped and feared.

In more recent years historians have become more interested in the local and the social, and the advent of the camera opened the eyes of a few photographers to the possibilities of recording contemporary history through the lens. To begin with there was a formality about that sort of record, too; and even when the subject no longer had to stand unnaturally still, the resulting picture was of a second, frozen in time. But add to the picture the human voice and there is a new dimension that increases its value on an almost infinite scale. The milkmaid may pose on a fine day, her cows and her pail at the ready, but it takes the human voice to remind the listener that milking in the pouring rain was a miserable experience and the only possible protection was a sack draped across the milker's shoulders.

It is the human voice, with its individual inflexions, its localised accent, and its innate ability to convey by tone what the best command of words cannot do, that brings our most recent history to life. And it is just that recent history that is otherwise so elusive. Whatever improvements came with free and universal education did not bring in their wake much desire to record the ordinary and the obvious, though the Mass-Observation initiative of the late 1930s found a significant number of people ready to contribute to what came to be an invaluable picture of wartime Britain that complemented the work of the artists of the Recording Britain project. The idea of the Somerset Voices initiative was not, of course, the wartime expedient of recording a threatened way of life and threatened buildings in face of possible Nazi destruction, but instead to preserve them both from the depredations of age on memory.

The new world that emerged from the Second World War is well within what is commonly called living memory, and yet young readers will find it almost incredible that houses did not have mains water and sanitation, gas or electricity.

The now common acceptance that fridges, freezers, radios and televisions, washing machines and their like are absolutely essential for living, let alone the growing belief that natural commodities are somehow created in supermarkets, is a sad reflection of a generation that has somehow failed to speak and of its successor for not wanting to listen. But perhaps successor generations do not listen to each other; our grandparents are the guardians of our past.

And this book, and the huge collection of recordings of which it is a tiny sample, is exactly that: the memories of the guardians of our past. Here are people who grew up with candles and tin baths and outside loos and who could remember, as clearly as if it were yesterday, the excitement of adequate light at the flip of a switch, the luxury of instant warm water, and the comfort of a water closet without the expedition into the garden.

Readers will find that these extracts jog memories. My grandfather rented a dairy before taking a farm tenancy; his elder daughter, my aunt, made cheese for a farmer at Marston Magna. When the family farm, a mile or so over the county boundary in Dorset, was sold in 1947 a carthorse was disposed of as well as two tractors, a reaper-binder, various horse-drawn bits of machinery, a long-abandoned cream-separator, a small butter churn and dozens of other items whose like are now displayed in farm museums. By the age of nine I had driven one of the tractors, broken up cattle cake in the decorticator and ridden another horse to the blacksmith.

In the farmhouse we had mains water, a proper bath and toilet and generated enough electricity for lighting that, the farmstead and two cottages, but my grandmother cooked with paraffin and used a copper to heat water for bathing and washing clothes. Staying with other members of the family involved rather alarming visits to evil-smelling sheds in the garden where squares of newspaper hung on rusty nails; a back kitchen with a bare concrete floor, a modern bath installed in the middle and no fastening on the door; and a pig dripping blood on the dairy floor. I was living through a domestic revolution without knowing it. I will tell my granddaughter all about it.

The memories in this book and in the whole collection are of another world; of smaller towns, of self-sufficient villages, from which many never ventured far. It was a world of simple pleasures, home-made entertainment; of lives lived close to the land and to nature. These are voices of a special time and of special places; they speak nostalgically, though in truth life was tough, sometimes very hard indeed.

And congers on the seashore, salmon and elvers in the rivers, withies, teasels, flax, horse-hair weaving and paper-making, lush grass, butter and cheese together can only be Somerset. And Margot's memory of being surprised in her bath by the butcher is a gem!

Robert Dunning

INTRODUCTION

T HE ORAL ARCHIVE, a collection of recordings of Somerset people, is held by the Somerset Heritage Service at the Somerset Rural Life Museum in Glastonbury. The collection was begun in 1973 by the then Keeper of Rural Life, Kate Walters, and was continued by her successors, Martyn Brown and Mary Gryspeerdt. The newly formed Friends of the Abbey Barn, later renamed the Friends of the Somerset Rural Life Museum, were actively involved from 1979. Ann Heeley, who was a founding member of the Friends, together with other Friends, started recording and transcribing the spoken word. Since then the collection has increased to more than 600 recordings, primarily with the assistance of the Friends' Oral Archive Group.

In 2004 the Oral Archive received funding from the Heritage Lottery to digitise the collection, with a view to making it more accessible to the public via CDs held at Glastonbury and the Somerset Heritage Centre in Taunton. It was decided to produce a publication of highlights from the Archive to bring this fascinating collection to a wider public.

The majority of the men and women recorded were born in Somerset or lived most of their lives in the county, and there is a diversity of background and status, with people living in cottages, farmhouses and manor houses in villages and in towns. Those interviewed came from across the county including west Somerset, the Quantock villages, the Levels and the Moors, the coast, central and south Somerset and the Mendip hills.

This publication has been drawn entirely from the Oral Archive and records people talking about their lives in agriculture, rural industries and crafts as well as their social activities and home life. The book has three themes: At Work, At Home and In the Villages and the Towns. To select recordings was extremely difficult; there are so many wonderful memories and experiences. In all cases we have tried to change as little as possible in the extracts in order to keep the words close to the original. However, in some instances we have altered the order of the wording to make it more easily readable.

For each person we have given the date of birth and the parish to which they refer. In certain circumstances we have not been able to use a direct extract, because it was not possible to obtain permission, and therefore the words are set out in narrative form. The illustrations have been drawn from personal collections, the Somerset Heritage Service and other museum archive collections. Some images relate directly to the subject but in many cases it has not been possible, so we have used photographs which we feel are appropriate.

We would like to thank all those family members we have visited or contacted, who have kindly given permission for the use of extracts and photographs and for all their help and generous assistance.

We hope we have given a glimpse into rural life in Somerset during the twentieth century. We have immensely enjoyed all the work in reading and listening to the collection, and only regret that we were unable to include many more wonderful memories on numerous other subjects.

Ann Heeley, Louise Clapp and Liz Snelgrove
April 2010

Men at Kilve posing with eels and celebratory drinks as they display their catch of conger eels.

CHAPTER ONE
AT WORK

SOMERSET ENCOMPASSES a range of geographical features which has influenced the working lives of its inhabitants. The poorer soils on the hills, the rich pastures of the low-lying Levels and Moors and the coastal strip by the Bristol Channel, each evolved specialist occupations. Hence memories come from strawberry growers, farmers, cheese-makers, cider-men, peat diggers, ditchers, basket-makers, fishermen and craftsmen.

Within the limits of their surroundings and before the advent of modern transport, many working people carried on the traditional work of generations of their families. As the century progressed, and especially after World War II, this began to change.

Butter, cream and cheese

In the early years of the twentieth century it was common practice to begin farming by renting a dairy. For the first year or two a man may have rented only ten cows and if successful then he would move on to rent a larger dairy. Advertisements for renting dairies appeared in the local newspapers usually in the late winter. Eventually enough money would have been saved to take up a farming tenancy or buy a farm. Sidney White (b.1890) started farming in this way.

> A lot of farmers let their dairies to a dairyman and the dairyman had to make the best use he could, making the cheese, and pay the farmer so much a year for the rent of the cows. In fact when I started I paid £11 a year for twenty-two cows. When I was married first I went to Sock Farm, Chilthorne, rented the farm, twenty-two dairy farm, and then after I'd been there two years I saw an advert for a dairy to let down on the Forde Abbey estate, and that was forty cows.
>
> The cheese was my produce. My wife was doing it. She did all the slave work. I did the talking, which was a very good arrangement! We was both consulting one another as to what we would do next. In fact when we got married first she said to me 'Now

*Sidney White (4th from front)
hand milking with his wife,
Gertie, and other staff at
Sock Dennis Farm, Ilchester.*

*Hand-milking out in the fields at
Ken Stuckey's farm at Kingston
Seymour.*

which way shall I make the cheese? Your way or my way?' I said 'Oh make it your way, my dear', and she said 'No, I've been thinking, you've had more experience than I have, perhaps we'd better make it your way.' And that's what we did.

I stayed there four years, and then I came back and I bought Sock Dennis Farm and that was a derelict farm. There were ant hills there as high as that! Sock Dennis was terrible clay soil, and I went there in 1918 and I left there in 1940 so I always said I'd done twenty years penal servitude and I hadn't committed a crime, so I felt free to clear out.

Milk produced by the dairy cows on farms in Somerset was either made into butter and cheese on the farm or transported by rail to dairies in one of the large towns, or sold locally. Later, in the 1930s, the dairies provided their own transport and collected the milk direct from the farm. Ken Stuckey (b.1911), of Kingston Seymour, had such an arrangement with a dairy.

Delivery vans from Hucker's Dairy in Chew Stoke.

We used to hand-milk perhaps forty-five or fifty cows between five of us. We used to go out in the fields and milk all summer and we drove the horse and cart with the seventeen gallon churns, strainer and five gallon buckets. Then we would bring the milk home and cool it with water from the well. Each day we drove the churns to Yatton station to be put on the Nestlé milk train going to Chippenham. There was quite a slump in the mid 1930s when the milk prices dropped. I remember one summer all my father was getting was about four pence a gallon for his milk and that's about two and half pence in today's money.

Women undertook the dairy work and made clotted cream and butter. Excess over the family requirements would be sold in the local shops or markets. The making of clotted cream by scalding was a common practice in many farmhouse dairies. Ernest Hucker (b.1915), from Chew Stoke, recalled that his mother made and sold clotted cream.

Ernest Hucker, dairy farmer, of Fairseat Farm, Chew Stoke.

She used to make the cheese and also butter, and before we had the dairy built she used to scald cream on the old copper in the back kitchen of the house. When we started the milk round in '32 we immediately advertised ourselves as selling clotted cream coming from the country and we bought some pans from Cooper and Sons, and they supplied all the necessary utensils. She used to spread the milk and leave it for so many hours and then she used to get the boiler going, same as a wash day. We used to put laths across and put the pans on the laths so they would just be in the water. It was a long drawn out process.

We knew when to take it off, when it was crusting on top, then it had to be cooled down. In the summer time it was a difficult process; you had to get it right cool before you could skim off the cream with a skimmer. You didn't get much cream from two gallons. It made lovely soft clotted cream.

Before butter churns became widely used in the farmhouse dairies, butter was made by hand using large pans. Phyllis Jones (b.1918), who lived on a farm in Burrowbridge, recalled her mother making butter. This continued on some small farms until the 1950s where the expense of a butter churn could not be justified.

Forming the butter into shapes using butter 'hands' during a demonstration at the Somerset Rural Life Museum.

On Tuesdays we always used to make the butter. That was a busy day because we had about 20 pounds or 30 pounds of cream, perhaps more, all according how your cows was milking. But before you stirred your cream, you had to 'spall' your hands because your cream did stick to your hands. Well, that was you had to dip them in boiling water, rub them with salt, and then wash them in cold water, and then stir your cream by hand. Then it would come very easy in the winter, but in the summer you might be stirring all day before you could get it come. If it got hot you couldn't get it to turn — sometimes you could never get it to turn. In the summer we used always to use earthenware, we did, for to make the butter; it used to come a bit quicker in earthenware. In the winter we used to use the brass pan, but we didn't have so much cream then.

You'd got your cream all made up into butter. Then you'd draw off that skimmed milk what would come out of it. Then you got buckets of cold, cold water from your pump and you washed that four or five times to get all the butter-milk out of it. Then you put salt in it, a little bit to make it just taste, sprinkle it around. Oh, and then you keep squeezing it to get the water out of it.

Then we used to have the pats and pat it all up and make it in different shapes; we had acorns and different things. Then we used to have great, big wicker baskets, pack it in and put the greaseproof paper over it and then take it to the market in the shops on Wednesday to sell it.

A large proportion of the milk in Somerset was made into cheese before World War II. The milk came mainly from Shorthorn cattle and was of good quality; the quality of milk could vary from month to month according to the kind of food the cattle eat and the health of the cows. The best milk for cheese-making contained a high percentage of fat and protein.

Cheese-making was an important skill before raw milk could be transported into towns, so the children in a farming family were taught the long, slow process of making cheese. The dairy had to be spotlessly clean at all stages, so that no taints affected the finished cheese. Walter

An 'improver' cheese girl taking instructions from Gertie White of Sock Dennis Farm, Ilchester, c.1920.

Baber (b.1904), of Chewton Mendip, explained that many farmers' daughters wanted to learn how to make cheese and every year his mother had a pupil.

We always made cheese and practically every year we had a pupil. There was reams of farmers' daughters around looking for a job like that where they could learn from a good maker. In fact Mr Tate at Wells, the wine and spirit merchants, he used to travel round to practically all the farmers around Christmas time looking for orders and he used to have a bag full of names, young ladies who would like to learn the job. That's how they did come to you.

They'd stay perhaps two years; the first year they didn't handle it very much, you see, and the second year they would take on more responsibility. Father used to say every girl he had as a cheese-maker went off and got married. It was what the young men in those days wanted, everybody who was a cheese-maker of any consequence, and who could they find better for a wife than one who had been trained in the real art of cheese-making?

Caerphilly cheese curds being packed into the moulds at Walnut Tree Farm, Heath House, 1987.

Between April and October, when they were eating grass, the majority of farms with dairy cows made Cheddar cheese. Caerphilly cheese was made during the winter months when the cows were eating hay. Albert Wilkins (b.1894) and his father operated this familiar pattern of cheese-making on the family farm in High Ham.

> Caerphilly cheese, through the winter, used to be took to Highbridge Market, and that used to be sent over in Wales to the miners. He used to go on his own there, but Cheddar cheese, wherever you had to take them, you had to haul them on the horse and wagons. You take on perhaps two or three ton a time.
> The cheese you sold to the dealer, he come and buy them there, then you take them to his place, where he want them trucked — put on the rail and sent somewhere else. One year we made a lot. We had a crest, a government crest, put on the cheese. Some of them went to Spain, and some went to London, to different hotels.
> Now we had to send them separately, put them in baskets, withy baskets, what they make round, you know, in the moors.

Levels and Moors

The Somerset wetlands are ideal for water-loving willow trees, their supple stems used by early man; late Iron Age willow basket fragments were found on the site of Glastonbury Lake Village. From the nineteenth century withies were grown commercially and used in the making of salmon and eel traps, coracles, baskets, furniture and coffins. During World War II withies were woven into panniers — large baskets — used for dropping items, ranging from food to ammunition, by parachute from aircraft into occupied Europe.

Cutting of the crop was undertaken during the winter months after the first frost caused the leaves to drop from the stem. Edward Male (b.1922) grew withies in Kingsbury Episcopi.

> For most of my life I cut withies by hand with a hook in the winter. After you cut them you carted them to the ditch. We had a boat to row them out and then you hired somebody to haul them from there to your home. The moors in those days were too wet. Then we sorted them out: the ones you wanted for white you put in the withy pit standing in water about 3 or 4 inches deep. We had concrete pits, so they were nice and clean when they came out. They stayed there until the sap came up and you could strip them and they would be white. If you wanted them buff you had to boil them for about eight or nine hours.
> My father had a boat made — it was really a punt with a flat bottom. We used to

Albert Hembrow cutting withies with a hook.

Loading cut withies onto a boat.

load it till it was about that much from sinking, down to the rim. You could put in about fifty or fifty-five bundles at 7 foot long. You had to use a pole to get in the withy beds and pole vault over the ditches. I could jump across a 12 foot ditch.

Burrowbridge, North Petherton, North Curry, Kingsbury Episcopi, Langport and Stoke St Gregory were the main withy-growing areas. William Palmer (b.1883) from Athelney, near Burrowbridge, started working in a family business with his uncles at the age of eleven, making wicker chairs and baskets. He continued for seventy-eight years apart from two years in the army during World War I.

William Palmer, basket-maker of Stoke St Gregory, with some of the chairs he made, in 1968.

When I started there was very little buff willow, it was mostly white work — Champion Rod and Black Spaniard — and then they introduced Black Maul, which is a better willow for working with as it grew from year to year. There were thousands of chairs made in buff, all different patterns and sizes. Some of our customers were from London; you would send down two dozen or ten dozen chairs or whatever you had made.

We used the peeled buff willows, all peeled singly by hand, to make the chairs; made the arms and legs with two year willow sticks, while the seat, back and sides were one year old rods. I worked a twelve hour day for myself, perhaps until eight and nine o'clock at night. Before the last war there wasn't the demand for chairs so I made baskets, the old fishing baskets with four legs. Holidays? I never been on holiday, never been to a dance or the cinema!

Aubrey Hill (b.1935) joined his father basket-making after learning the trade of a carpenter. The workshop in North Petherton was rented and as the business grew they moved to Bridgwater to larger workshops.

We were making pigeon baskets for quite a few years and then the railways stopped carrying livestock, and it went over to these big transporters carrying the pigeons, and we made some baskets for them as well, but it gradually faded out. Other things came in like the fishing baskets and picnic baskets. We made thousands and thousands for people like Antler luggage.

I had a phone call one day and the voice said, 'Can you make large baskets?' and I said, 'Yes, we can make anything,' being very big-headed about it! The guy turned up with a balloon basket on a trailer and said, 'Can you make one of these?' and that was about twenty-five years ago.

Aubrey Hill in March 2003 making a willow coffin in the workshop at Bridgwater.

Robert Chambers studying a rough block of willow prior to shaping it into a cricket bat at his workshop near Taunton cricket ground, October 2001.

Traditional willow cricket bat-making declined in Somerset but was re-started in 1987 by an Australian bat-maker with two partners. Robert Chambers (b.1979) began as an apprentice and in 2000 purchased the business which is now in a workshop near the Somerset cricket ground in Taunton. He uses a triangular wedge or cleft of seasoned solid willow wood from a mature tree.

Little bit of a strange one! I was contacted out of the blue by Somerset careers office. They said there was an apprenticeship going in Taunton. They didn't actually tell me what it was for, but they just said it was on the subject of woodwork. So I came for an interview and thought 'Aah! That is interesting, not many people do that!' It just went from there.

The willow merchants have big monopolies with farmers who grow willow for

them. It's about a ten year cycle. The willow merchants will then go and harvest the trees and sell it on to us. It's chopped down into manageable blocks. Basically, from the rectangular block of willow we have to fashion that down to a workable size and so what we do is use a combination of machines to do this. We spend an awful lot of time sanding it down by hand. We've also got a horse's shin bone which gives it a final polishing. Now, that's been soaked in linseed oil for six months and it just polishes the wood off nicely. The handle is made of a Malaysian cane. It's got three or four rubbers sandwiched in between. We have to rasp the handles to take out all the bumps and get a nice oval shape, and spoke-shave the shoulders smooth.
Our cheapest bat is £155 and that goes up to about £245 for the top of the range. That's determined from the quality of the wood, which generally means the more grains in a piece, the better the performance, therefore the higher price.

In other parts of the wetlands peat-digging took place, especially in the moors around Glastonbury. The peat was dug in the spring and allowed to dry during the summer months before being taken by horse and cart round the towns and villages and sold as fuel for fires. It is now mainly used as a soil conditioner in gardens. Henry Whitcombe (b.1900), of Westhay, used to dig and sell peat.

We generally cut the peat from about April until the end of August because if you cut in the winter time the frost used to take the burning value out of the peat. We used to cut it ten inches long, eight inches high and nine inches deep. The blocks

A man cutting peat blocks and lifting them up to a woman who lays them out in rows.

or mumps were laid out on the ground and then cut up into threes known as bricks. The men cut the peat and women used to hyle the bricks into a shape to allow the air to circulate. A hyle was fourteen peat bricks and they had to be left to dry for about a fortnight. When fairly dry the bricks were gathered into tall heaps about eight feet high called ruckles.

I sold twenty peat blocks for sixpence, but I mind the time they were ten blocks of peat for a penny. Every house and cottage used to burn peat in those days. I used to go to Highbridge, Berrow, Burnham and Brent Knoll once a week and later when I had a motor lorry I used to go to Taunton, Winscombe and Weston-super-Mare with peat to earn my living.

Drainage, sea walls and fishing

In the Somerset wetlands drainage is essential to enable efficient farming. Fields are surrounded by six-foot wide boundary ditches which drain into the larger rhynes; both require regular maintenance. Charlie Keirle (b.1916) worked on the Levels around Stoke St Gregory and Burrowbridge keeping the ditches and rhynes in good order.

I was carter on the lands right up 'til the time the horses went out, but when the tractors came in, I didn't want anything to do with them, so automatically I went on the rhyne work in the Sedgemoor.

We used the staff hook and the shearing knife and the crook. Everything was done by hand. Always those three. I had a scythe that we made for ourself, which is so much better for bringing the grass up from the brink of the ditch. You only wants your staff hook and your shearing knife then to straighten your ditch out... you see, we used to be able to go over our old blacksmith years ago and don't matter what stem or anything, don't matter how crooky he was, he could always put that in, so long as you tell him which hand you were, left or right, he could always put that tool so as it was what you could use.

When we were doing the rhynes, 'n' there's two of us, we could do anything from thirty to forty ropes a day. Of course, in those days, they were done twice a year and 'twas just, the majority of the work, was the trimming of the banks. Owing to being done twice a year, you hardly had anything at all in the ditches to pull out, but now, today, course they're so much worse.

When I started first, we had about eightpence, ninepence a rope in old money. A week's wages, when I started on the rhynes was about thirty-six shillings a week.

*Charlie Keirle clearing
ditches on Sedgemoor.*

Farm workers at Moortown Farm, Curry Rivel, at the Langport and District annual ploughing match and hedging competition, pre 1930. The men are carrying their trademark spades and hooks and are wearing strong leather gloves.

Bert Peppard (b.1912) worked on a number of farms in the Aller and Othery area before starting to farm on his own. Clearing field drainage systems was very familiar to him.

> When I was fourteen I used to go up digging rhynes and ditches and I got paid about two shillings a rod, which was twenty foot. I scythed to cut the sides out first and then used shovels and cutting shovels and ditch knives to clean the ditches. An old chap with a donkey and cart hauled the tools that we needed to the ditches.

The field patterns in some places in Somerset are defined by the hawthorn hedges that extend into many thousands of miles. Farm workers were proud of their skills and hedging competitions were fiercely contested. The hedges were cut and laid by hand in the winter months and the smoke from the bonfires would be seen curling towards the sky on cold frosty days. Ken Stuckey (b.1911), of Kingston Seymour on the Levels, explained the importance of good hedges.

> There were hedges everywhere. Nearly all the hedges are hawthorn and there are miles and miles of them and must have been planted in Napoleonic times. They make wonderful windbreaks because we are near the sea and we get a lot of cold sea air coming in. Another thing that has gone now are the elm trees. I usually find that where there were outlying cottages in the fields they would plant elm trees to protect them.

Parishes on the Bristol Channel coast, which included Ken Stuckey's farm, had the responsibility of keeping the earthen sea wall in good repair, solid and firm, so no water would penetrate into the low-lying fields.

> The maintenance of the sea walls was the responsibility of the owners of all the properties in Kingston Seymour. All these sections were marked off by stones and showed the initials of the person whose responsibility it was and a record was kept by the Commissioners of Sewers of the Yatton Division and they inspected them once or twice a year. That's how the sea wall was kept up from about 1630 until it was taken over by the Somerset River Board in 1937.
> We had the longest stretch, which was 40 lugs which was forty times 5 yards, and in March time we would haul up turves and pack them in weak places where cattle would stand on top of the sea wall. In the late summer, in September, we removed any weeds and other obstructions.
> The earthen sea wall was about 8 feet high and 6 feet wide and sloped down towards the sea which lapped against it and there's no doubt if there was a very

high tide the sea came over the wall, which was grassed over. When the earthen wall was replaced by a concrete one, they made the sides too upright so it took a hammering from the tide.

People living in parishes with boundaries along the sea and rivers were skilled in catching fish in a variety of ways. The fish were an important part of their diet especially for those on low incomes. Grace Parish (b.1919), a farmer's daughter, recalled salmon butts, wicker nets, in the River Parrett at Stretcholt.

Now there were fishermen, down at Stretcholt, that is the hamlet of Pawlett, fishermen who would fish the river for dabs, eels, shrimps. In the salmon season they put down things they call butts, with big open front and it runs back to nothing. So the salmon would go in and

A fisherman checking the salmon butts on the shores of the Bristol Channel.

when the tide was going out, they would always catch them, you see, the salmon could not come out. They have got about fifty of these butts in a line, staked.

But if you want to go out in a boat, and have a net and you see a salmon — and they scoop them up, you see, and catch them like that. Another way of catching them, when the tide goes out it just leaves the sand uncovered. The people, they will go down right down over the muddy bank and walk along these sand dunes and sometimes they pick up perhaps half a dozen.

The salmon season: that's from May till July. I suppose it is when they are running up to spawn.

West of the River Parrett estuary, on the Stert flats, Brendan Sellick (b.1934) of Stolford, followed a family tradition of fishing with a mud-horse, a device pushed over the mud at low tide to the rows of nets in the fishing grounds. The shrimp nets were set on poles six feet high and the individual nets stretched between the poles. These nets had mouths five feet square tapering back about six feet and were tied to a short post. The catch became densely packed into the tapered end which was untied and emptied into a sieve for sorting.

In Bridgwater Bay as a whole there was a terrible lot of activity in the fishing but here was the principal place, at Stolford, that used to catch enormous amounts of

Brendan Sellick, aged 17, pushing the mudhorse across the soft mud of Stert Flats on the shores of the Bristol Channel. He started helping his father as a ten-year-old and became full time at fifteen.

shrimps and stuff; and there was a lot of people who did it, but then when I started there were about four or five different people doing it. Then up to twenty years ago there was three o' us and then fifteen year ago there's just me – I'm the last one.

We've never used a boat here, we've always used the old-fashioned mud-horse that's been going back to Roman times; for hundreds of years we've used the same implement. We call it the mud-horse or the sledge and it's just a simple device that we've been using all these years. Never had anything different and we still use it today. We don't use that to catch the fish, we use the implement to go from the beach across the mud flats to the fishing grounds, which is about a mile to two miles off shore, right out on the sand bars.

There was no other way of getting there, only by scooting across the top, so we've always used the mud-horse to get from A to B across a mile of soft treacherous mud. We go out two hours to low water enabling us to get two hours work done and then if you haven't done your work you have to throw it back or get back because once the tide turns, well then, you've gotta come back, 'cos the tide come in, it creeps in behind you and it floods the whole area in no time at all.

We've had a good cod season all through the winter, and sprats, whiting, conger, skate — we catch a lot of skate — a few dover soles and plaice, flounder, whiting, a few gurnard, a lot of dogfish, a few sharks, shrimps and prawns. Of course we don't get the shrimps in abundance like we used to get, but there it is, we still get quite a nice lot.

We take baskets and nets out and whatever we can put in the nets and in the baskets. We pack them onto the mud-horse and scoot back across, pedalling with your feet across the mud flats; that's why I say it's hard work so you have to be fit enough to do it.

Heavy horses

Horses were a vital part of all farming until tractors universally took their place during and after World War II. Farmers with breeding mares usually belonged to the local branch of the Shire Horse Society which organised for a man to come and travel round the district with a stallion. Maurice Hasell (b.1918), from Bishop Sutton, recalled the arrival of the stallion at his father's farm.

Horses were used before we had the tractor. We had six or eight heavy horses; I think about three mares. Shire horses, big horses. He used to breed horses. The stallion used to come all round the farms. I think it came from Peterborough; I'm

not sure, mind. They would appoint farms who would agree to keep a stallion overnight, and then he would use the mare. He'd walk with this great big horse, a massive thing he was, I can see him now! He had a leather strap and his hair would be all plaited up with ribbons, all along the top and his tail. He had a big strap go under his belly, I don't know what that was for. And I don't know how far he would walk the next day, but he would walk to the next farm the next day, you see, and go into other farms all the way.

We usually rear the colts on — two years to the halter, you know — and any we didn't want he'd sell those at Backwell Fair.

When horses were the main source of transport and of power on the farm, the blacksmith's shop was a very important feature of the village. In Nether Stowey Bill Redding (b.1908) started working in Lime Street with his father when he was fourteen years old. His father, William, started at the age of eleven. The making and fitting of horseshoes was their main livelihood, using the basic tools of anvil, tongs, hammers, chisel and poker.

Shire mares and their spring born foals at Middle Ivythorn Farm, Walton, prior to leading them down to Tor Fair in Glastonbury to sell the foals.

We did make shoes in those days. We had to make them all, me and father together, for many years until shoes were made in the factories. One thing, you can't beat your own made shoes.

It was hard work in my early years — had to do all the sledge work. There were great cart horses we had to be under, over a ton in weight. That was all day long. If you had the shoes ready, you could always reckon to do a horse an hour, that's the big cart horses. Lighter ones you would do them quicker. In winter time when it's slippery roads, they'd walk their horse for frost nails — that's steel nails put outside the shoe to stop them slipping. I have put nails into horses' shoes at 6 o'clock in the morning, doing it by candle light in the dead of winter before the horses went on to Bridgwater.

Opposite page: *Bill Redding working at his forge.*

The village saddler was essential when horse power prevailed. Tom Ware (b.1925) started working with his father in Nether Stowey. The major part of their work involved repairing harness for the heavy horses; they used to get their material — leather, hemp, flax and wax — from wholesalers in Bristol and Walsall.

We were repairing cart harness for Shire horse-work. Heavy work: cart collars, saddles, breeching. The horses used to wear them until five o'clock at night. Take off the collar and saddles, they were all covered in sweat. And the breeching that goes under the tail, you can imagine what that was like! We used to repair them in the evening, stitch through the mess and muck. Made the wax thread ourselves, what we called four cord hemp. Hemp for cart work, flax for bridle work. No wages until I started courting; my father couldn't afford to pay me any wages.

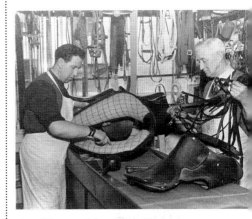

Tom Ware with his father, Walter, at their saddlers' workshop in Nether Stowey.

Horses were vital to Bertie Bond (b.1927) who as a young boy helped his father on his farm in North Barrow at the beginning of World War II. The family lived on a predominantly grass farm and had to plough old pasture land with cross-bred horses to satisfy the ever-increasing demand for cereals. Many farms in Somerset were forced to plough up land that in some cases was totally unsuitable because it was so wet, but grew excellent grass.

When the war years came we were detailed to plough up certain fields to grow wheat or whatever they wanted. My dad and somebody else went down and broadcast oats over the top of the furrows and the oats fell down between the furrows and then we dragged it and did the best we could and that's how we grew our first crop.

We had chain harrows for the grass land and a pair of heavy drags and our horses

Bob Hallett ploughing using a pair of heavy horses in Butleigh during the 1930s.

were cross-breds, known as halfway horses. These were horses that would trot up the road, go to market, pull a pair of chain harrows and a mower: active horses. Arable horses were heavy horses. They had good hairy legs and they were very muscley, steadier going, but used to pulling a lot heavier loads.

Froude Hill (b.1899) lived on a mixed farm in Fiddington. His father operated an eight year rotation system; roots, oats, wheat under-sown with clover, rye grass, a one year ley for spring grass, wheat, beans, wheat and back to roots. The ploughing was done by a team of horses as well as a Titan tractor purchased in 1917.

Mr Meaker that used to be at Fiddington, he said the last time he saw oxen ploughing on a field was that large field out there, and we have picked up the shoes there. We have never used them. We had eight or ten horses eating twenty or thirty acres of grass.

The ploughing was always done with three horses with a single furrow plough and they ploughed nearly an acre a day. We had the front horse trained so well that he would go without any reins with the carter speaking to him. Then, of course, the old carters would keep their plough going along exactly the same depth, about five and half inches, no matter what you said to them, because it was easier to go on exactly where it had been ploughed years before, and that tended to make a seal there. A neighbour farmer used to what they called 'strick up' the furrows; they'd have a little furrow to take the surface water off, but we never did it and when we

One of a pair of steam engines pulling a plough from side to side across a field at Tugrushing Corner, Butleigh. The wire connecting the engine to the plough is behind the men and the engine driver, Reg Masters, is standing by the machine.

A Titan tractor on a farm in Fiddington, 1917. These were imported from the USA in large numbers by the Ministry of Food Production as part of the efforts to feed World War I Britain. This was one of a small number allocated to Somerset.

had the tractors, there was no need of that because the tractors went deeper and different depths and the water would go down.

But then we had those steam cultivators in a rotation, once in six or seven years; they ripped it up deeper. We used to have the steam tackle from Dorset: one big engine at one end of the field and the other at the other to pull a cultivator. They used to come, five of them, four of them working and one waiting on them. And it kept one man hauling water to them to cope.

There was only one tractor in the district before the one that we had. It was a Titan. They had thirty gallons of water on the front of it to keep it cool. They pulled the plough with a chain. They were splendid tractors.

Planting and gathering

Peas were grown and regularly transported by train in baskets to the vegetable markets in London, Bristol and the Midlands. Ernest Jones (b.1908) remembered growing peas at Pratts Farm, North Petherton.

Three gypsy pea-pickers harvesting the crop in South Petherton, 1906, lifting the hellum for the camera. A visitor is posing with them.

My grandfather, with a Mr Joe West, were the pioneers of growing peas in the open fields. The soil in North Petherton is a very light sand, well drained, and the variety of peas grown was Early Eclipse, which was drilled into the fields around the two Christmases, 25th December to 6th January. There was what was called a pea drill where you would put the peas in at the top and you had a cup feed and they used to trickle down through into the ground.

The time we gathered peas in the open field, that is by women — some men but not many — on a day-work basis, you had what was considered to be the best of your pickers to go into the field first and make a path through. The women used to pick the peas in what was called 'pootches' that they made of linen, and they tied this pootch around their waist and they had to bend their backs to pick the peas. There would be as many probably in the early days as forty pickers in the field. They would be looked after with a ganger. When he saw that one picker had her pootch nearly full he would then say 'Bottoms up!' and that would mean every woman or man there would have to untie their pootch and the ganger would come along with willow baskets, which would hold around a bushel. These baskets, once they were full, the ganger would pick up some green hellum, the stuff that the peas grow on, and put it over the top and tie it down with string.

In the afternoon, 'round about four o'clock, you would get the carter come up with the horse and wagonette and they were taken into Bridgwater Station, destined to perhaps Birmingham, Bristol, Covent Garden, various places. You would get your orders to where to send them round about ten o'clock in the morning, when it was all done by telegram because not many farmers then had the telephone. If the weather got very, very bad, your women or your pickers were rather loathe even to go home because they wanted the money. I have seen, as a boy, my late father's pea pickers coming down the row with their great long skirts schrouching around with the wet and the dirt from the fields. They would go home and clean themselves up, ready for the next day.

The land on the south-facing slopes of the Mendip Hills was ideal for fruit and vegetable growing. Arnold Thomas (b.1912) was one of many smallholder strawberry growers in the Cheddar area. He joined his father when he left school and recalled the types of material used to keep the strawberries clean as they grew and ripened on the plants and also the experiments to find the right kind of containers for them. The fruit travelled by passenger train to various markets across the country.

The strawberry industry was started in Cheddar in the latter part of the 1800s by a

Young women and children with their baskets of strawberries c.1930.

Mr Stan Spencer, who grew the Royal Sovereign variety, which were very large and had a beautiful flavour. An uncle of mine picked the prize-winner of all England on our holding, for a strawberry weighing over four ounces. They named it 'St. Paul's Cathedral'. It was an outstanding strawberry and he won the prize in the *Daily Mail* for that year.

A problem they ran into in the early days was the fact that they found the strawberries used to get dirty by splashing from the rain. So they had quite a clever idea of cutting some of the heather from the Blackdown and also the bracken and they used to put this between the strawberries and that avoided the splashing but they found it was hard work and they couldn't get enough of it. After this, 'sparta grass waste from St Cuthbert's paper mill was tried and this was very successful. And then they used straw provided by farmers and that is still used. Nothing has been found to better it, except some cloche growers use black polythene.

They had quite a problem in the early years finding suitable containers but eventually managed to get some wicker basket-makers in Cheddar to make them some 12 pound baskets which were sent to market with the first cropping. But the problem was having to wait for them to be returned to pick the next lot of strawberries. Later the chipping machine was developed which chipped conifer logs; and the growers make their own four pound chip baskets.

David Sheldon (b.1929) followed his father and grandfather into the family business of vegetable and strawberry growing in Draycott. In the 1950s horses were still used on the land and the first job in the early morning was to go into the field and catch the horse. The horse and cart would take the picked strawberries to the local station and then by train on the

Covered chip baskets of strawberries being loaded on to a train at a station on the 'Strawberry Line'.

'Strawberry Line' to Yatton and from there to Newcastle, Hull, Edinburgh and Glasgow. Later in the same day the strawberries were sent to Liverpool, Bradford, Manchester and Accrington and to the Welsh Peninsula, Birmingham and Cardiff.

> And of course then they closed the branch line, I think it was about 1967, and for a little while the growers took their strawberries to Yatton and put them on the train. But that didn't last very long because road transport started to come in from the various towns up north. They were not able to give the service that Great Western railways did. And of course the strawberries didn't travel as well. You had this up and down movement all the way so the strawberries did not arrive in such good condition, and gradually the prices got lower and it became uneconomic for the growers. And that was another part of the demise of the strawberry industry.

A heavy rich clay without too much manure is favoured for the growth of teasels, providing a relatively lucrative crop on poor land. Teasels were used in the woollen cloth industry to 'raise the nap' or pile on high quality material such as that used for making uniforms. The Somerset teasels had firm and well-defined downward pointing hooks; those grown in France were softer. Reg Derrick (b.1914) described the crop from planting to harvesting when he was a young man. His father, grandfather and great-grandfather all grew teasels in West Hatch. When it was time to harvest, they had to use a proper teasel knife and gloves because they were very prickly, as well as a special coat and headwear because of the sap. They cut them into bundles of forty or fifty and put them on poles about ten feet high to dry, propped up into a wooden framework in the field or in a shed.

Flax can also grow on heavy clay soil, and has been grown in Somerset since medieval times especially in the Chard and West Coker areas. By the twentieth century it had diminished considerably but was revived when demand dictated. As part of the instructions to plough pasture land in World War I to grow crops, George Toose (b.1901) of Brympton D'Evercy recalled planting flax seed, and enlisting the help of girls in the National Service Corps to harvest the flax. The girls were taken to and from the fields in lorries, a jolly ride bumping over the country roads and were a welcome amusement for the folk who lived in and around Yeovil. The local people came in hundreds to see girls in breeches, living in tents; girls who were helping to make the aeroplanes that zoomed low over the fields of Somerset.

> During the First World War aeroplanes were in their infancy, and we had to grow flax to make the canvas for the aeroplane wings. I can remember going over Westland when they started making aeroplanes there: I saw these big rolls of canvas

Opposite page: *Teasels strung up on poles and propped together to dry.*

39

which women cut out, the right shape for the wings.

When we had to plough up permanent pasture, if we put it into cereals, there was a great risk of wireworm damage in the crop, but flax seemed to be fairly immune from wireworm, and that was the tempting crop, really, to grow. And it was put in, in April, and it grew fairly fast, and came out in a lovely blue flower. A field of flax was really a marvel, and then we had these girls, college girls mostly, I think, to pull it. They was brought round on lorries, dumped off at various farms and they spent the whole day pulling flax.

Cutting grass to make hay was a vital part of a livestock farmer's work. In wet seasons the grass would need to be turned several times before it was dry. It was then carted to the area where a hay rick or mow was to be made, to store the hay until the winter months when it was fed to dairy cows and other animals housed in buildings on the farm. George Toose also described hay making on his farm.

My father had hundreds of acres cut by the scythe in his younger days. They used to say a man could cut, on average, an acre a day with a scythe. If ten men went out into the field in the morning they'd cut ten acres of hay — grass, I should say. And also my father, in his younger days, he used to cut the wheat, oats and barley with a hook, hook and crook as they used to say, and tie it up by bonds.

We used to mow roughly seventy to eighty acres of permanent pasture for hay. Proper date to start mowing hay was eleventh of June. Old-fashioned idea I suppose. That was always the allotted date to start mowing. Then we used to pray for some nice hot sunny weather.

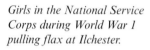

Girls in the National Service Corps during World War 1 pulling flax at Ilchester.

Eight men holding scythes to cut grass to be made into hay in West Somerset c.1930.

When I started first we had a two horse mowing machine which we used to start off at four o'clock in the morning; had to get up and get the horses in, get out in the field. I used to drive the mowing machine for a couple of hours and the carter used to sharpen the knives, ready for the rest of the day. And I'd go off cutting. He'd go home to breakfast during that time. When he'd finished sharpening his knives, I used to go home to breakfast and then he'd carry on mowing until the horses were wanted for turning hay elsewhere.

We had two swathe turners in those days; they'd go out and turn a ten acre field in a couple of hours, and that was left to dry for that day, and then turned again the next day, hoping to get it dry enough to cart. Well, that meant to say it was rewed up there, as we used to call it, with a ordinary hay rake, tip the handle; and then the wagons would come along, one man each side the wagon, pitching it up on the wagon with a long 'pitching pick'. And the man on the top, making the load of hay, when it was up as high as they could pitch it, sort of style, that was roped down and taken to the rick and unloaded loose on the rick, and the rick maker would build a rick with it.

Silage, another method of preserving cut grass, became popular after World War II. Silage can be made when the summer seasons are wet and farmers find it difficult to make hay as it is collected in when wilted, rather than dry. It was placed into a more or less air-tight pit, clamp or building especially erected for the purpose. In all storage methods the grass is covered. Dennis Baker (b.1922) made silage on his farm in Westhay.

We make perhaps ten acres of hay, but all the rest is silage. A bit of hay for young cattle and calves and a few off-lying cattle but for the most of the winter, most of the animals would be housed and all fed on silage. It is a much surer crop than hay. Hay is always a risky crop; you need three fine days and a nice day after you've cut it. No-one can guarantee that in England, so although everyone used to make hay, some of it was of very doubtful quality. Silage is much more consistent in quality. We mow the grass, and then we leave it for twenty-four hours so we don't get so much effluent which could cause pollution problems. We pick it up with a forage harvester which chops the grass up, and loaded into high-sided trailers; the grass is then put onto a big clamp. It has to be sealed down, covered by a plastic sheet and a few bales of straw or tyres to keep as much air out as possible because of the fermentation. If air gets in then the silage tends to heat up and it spoils.

Harvest time was when the heaviest work of the year took place but gradually in the late nineteenth century harvesting by scythe and sickle was replaced by small reaping machines. Many Somerset farmers in the early twentieth century were using machines known as trappers. Sidney Vaux (b.1900), from Wigborough, related how his father, before World War I, had harvested cereals using a trapper, driven by a boy sitting on one of the two horses pulling in tandem. When he was twelve or thirteen he had done that job himself but evidently had good reason to remember the experience.

Opposite page: Unloading second cut red clover and rye grass into the new wooden-sided silage clamp at Middle Ivythorn Farm, Walton in the early 1950s. The hayrick holds the first cut.

A group of harvesters at Parkhouse Farm, Kilve, with an early type of reaping machine known as a trapper c.1905.

I won't go into the details because the sweating of the horses made it very uncomfortable!

The man sits on the seat and he uses his foot with a flapper and he holds it up until he has got enough for a sheaf, releases his foot and it all drops out and a man comes along and ties it up by hand.

They would tie it by some of the grain itself; they were very quick. An interesting little story is: before they started, the six men that were going to tie it up had to divide the field into six, and nobody could count. So the old chap that took that job on had a stick and a knife and he counted in twenties. Every time he got to twenty yards he cut a notch. When he had completed around the field he divided the number of notches by six and then multiplied by twenty and so he got the correct stint for the men.

The first binder that came on this farm arrived the week that the First War broke out. It was a self-binder then — threw them out at the side.

After the harvest was gathered from the fields, local women and children were granted permission to enter harvest fields to glean any fallen heads of grain. Maurice Symes (b.1896) spoke about the system on his family farm in Coat, a hamlet of Martock. Farmers often referred to a field as being stitched, meaning that all the sheaves are standing to dry before carting and rick-making.

Women and children in a harvest field with stooks in Butleigh.

Stanley Adams and family with the threshing machine and team at Blagrove Farm, Butleigh Wootton.

We always left one and as long as that was there, there was no trespassing. But as soon as that was gone anybody that wanted to could go in and glean whatever corn was left for her. And they would tie it up and take it on down the mill and have it ground. They's take a pound of corn to be ground and bring back a bag of flour. After this was done you would turn the poultry out on it. They's keep what they would find there, especially in a dry summer, the corn that had dropped out. The poultry stayed there quite a long time without any feeding. Then some would let pigs out, pigs would gather up what was left there, see.

During the winter months threshing took place, where the cereal seeds were separated from the straw using a threshing machine powered by a steam engine or, later, a tractor. Farmers hired the threshing tackle for a couple of days to thresh or thrash a rick of corn. Dick Vearncombe (b.1898) recalled the process on his family's farm in Butleigh.

Old country, everyone used to call it 'drashing'.
You used to get the engine driver come six o'clock in the morning, to get up steam, and you used to take eleven men to do the job properly because you have one man

feeding, one man cutting binds and three on the rick to keep the thing supplied with corn. The people that were feeding the thrashing machine, there was an art, you see. Every sheaf would go in with the ears the same way all the time. And you'd want somebody keeping back the dust and the keffing as we used to call it — that's the ails from the ears of wheat or barley or whatever it was — and it used to be put back in a great big heap and hauled out afterwards. And then you used to want two or three people pitching straw away from behind the tie-er from the thrasher.

Barley in those days we used to thrash, and that used to go in the rick loose, and that took three men to keep away the barley straw that had been put on the rick and that was always pitched up — hard work. Wheat used to be tied in bundles; I don't know how much, I expect it would be about eight to the hundredweight.

We had to provide coal for the engine, and of course water, which was a big necessity then. We used to supply the engine driver and the feeder, either ways what they used to call grub money, or give them their meals.

Christine Smith (b.1924) was originally from Fulham and joined the Women's Land Army with a friend in 1942. They were both asked if they would be prepared to do field work in Pilton, Somerset. Christine and the other land girls got to know some of the local families in their spare time when they cycled to other villages. Some of the girls married local men, and never returned home.

I'd never set eyes on Somerset! We arrived at Shepton Mallet and there was this open lorry with some straw in it and we just sort of fell down the hills from Shepton, down to Steanbow farm. And it was just opened as a hostel then; smell of new paint and the yard was all in mud. And that I think was our first job, shovelling up this mud to clean the yard.

I think it was twelve field workers. But Steanbow opened as a training centre for milkers, apart from the field work. The training people came down from Cannington and they trained these hand milkers.

We had a cook — from that point of view we didn't look after ourselves — but we did our own washing and ironing. We had to pay, of course, out of our money for the keep. This had come under the War Agricultural Committee, so we were paid by them. When we'd finished it was no more than £3 a week.

Well, we did all field work that any other farm worker would do; feed for the cattle, and of course when the harvest came we had to do the old-fashioned type of harvesting. We all had to drive a tractor and did the hauling work.

Land girls' threshing team at Steanbow, Pilton, May 1943.

Combine harvesters were used in Somerset after World War II, replacing the self-binder which all but disappeared by the late 1960s. Clifford Hill (b.1904) had one of the early combines in 1946 at North Newton.

Just after the war we had the first combine. We thought it was an advantage being able to thrash the corn as you cut it — from having to cut it, and haul it in, put it in a rick and thrash it again. We got the permit to get this combine; it was an Oliver Combine from America. Well, eventually it came and it was all in boxes. They sent somebody and we put it together on the farm, and it was too wide: it cut eight feet, but it stuck out at one side, so we had to dismantle it with a trolley.

It was engine driven, and pulled by a tractor. Someone had to ride on the combine to regulate the height; you could do it with wheel like a ship's wheel, you know, with the spokes!

Nobody objected to it, oh no. Of course, for the first year every time we went out you always had an audience, all the local people would come and see it working.

It cost about four hundred and fifty pounds, that was without the trolley. But I had to give more than that for mine, I know. Somebody had it you know, wouldn't use it.

The Oliver combine harvester on West Newton Farm in North Newton.

Crafts

Some farmers grew a long-stemmed variety of wheat for thatching. Thatched houses can be found in many Somerset villages and there are still a few thatchers working in the county. The Wright family in Compton Dundon have been thatchers for four generations. Mark Nicholls (b.1965) and Adrian Dunster (b.1963) trained as thatchers and worked with the Wright family. Thatching is done throughout the year although wind and very heavy rain can stop the process. The old worn thatch is never completely taken off; it is prepared and new wads of tied straw are carefully placed on top of the old to form a new roof which will last about twenty-five years.

> You have to make a firm bed in front of you all the time. You dress the old roof to make it firm and even with a drifter. Then you lay your new thatch on top and spar it in. We use willow spars on the ridge and hazel on the coat which are twisted to form a peg about fourteen inches long. When we do a ridge we call it a step-up ridge. Most people use the old variety of straw called Huntsman, which is long with a hollow stem. We thatch all the year round. It's the winter really that is the worst time; it's cold, bitter, and of course the reed has always got to be watered to work on the roof. As you can imagine, straw is very slippery. If you had a wad of straw on the roof it would just slip off again. We use a tub to dip them in before we use them.

Bert Richards and Harold Wright, sparmakers, in the Wright's yard.

48

Dennis Wright stooking sheaves of thatching wheat in Compton Dundon, 1988.

The motorbike and sidecar that the Burgess family used for bread deliveries, outside their shop in Porlock.

At the age of three Dennis Corner (b.1926) moved to the home of his maternal grandparents who were bakers in Porlock. When he left school Dennis joined his grandfather, Isaac Burgess, and his uncles in their thriving business. They ran a shop and café and two bakers' rounds covering Porlock and the surrounding area. Dennis's grandfather delivered bread by horse and cart, then with a motorbike and sidecar before two vans were purchased. During the war commodities were short and it was difficult to supply bread, buns, rolls and cakes to every customer.

Various sorts of flours: soft flour for cakes, and then very strong flour for bread. The best flour of all came from Canada — Manitoba wheat. Everybody wanted white bread but during the war they made, I think they called it a National loaf which was not, it was off-white, but then we could also make brown bread. Hovis only made brown bread, I think, in those days — special loaf which was the wholegrain toasted apparently.

The wheat flour we used to use: we had a loft above, and we used to put it in a hopper, and the bags were 140 pound bags which we called a half sack because when they used to come in the real sacks years ago they were 280 pounds but they did cut them down in size because so many men injured themselves carrying them. We used to let it down through this hopper into the dough machine. It was basically flour, water, yeast and salt and we used to put a little bit of lard in with it. Nowadays they put all sorts of things in bread.

And on a very cold winter's morning, people would come to the shop, the bread wasn't ready. 'Oh, what happened? You overslept?' and no, it wasn't anything like that, you know. It just wouldn't rise and even with the bakehouse you could be cold. We used to wear jerseys in the wintertime.

The West Country climate and soil produced good quality cider apples which were grown in orchards on most farms until the 1940s. Increasingly since that date cider orchards have been removed in favour of more profitable crops, but a number of commercial enterprises still rely on Somerset apples. Cuthbert Rose (b.1907) was a cider maker from the Wedmore area.

We needed thirty hundredweights to two tons of apples to make what we call a 'cheese', and you really want about six people. One dealing with the bags of apples, pouring the apples out into the bushel basket; someone else who lifts that basket up and keeps the apple mill fed. The mill crushes them. Then you want someone with a shovel at the mill to shovel the crushed apples, the pomace, out onto the bed of the press. Then you want one, preferably two, chaps building the cheese so they can

arrange each lissom or layer of apple pomace on the bed with a layer of straw, reed as we call it. Each lissom is four or five inches thick, and we usually build up about seven or eight lissom to a cheese. Even without any pressure at all, by the time we have put up a cheese, we have probably run out about forty odd gallons of cider which comes out solely under the weight of the cheese itself.

As far as varieties are concerned, in many of our old orchards here we couldn't even put a name to a lot of the sorts. We know them by old names such as 'hangdowns', 'moonshines', 'sheepnoses', that sort of thing. Whether they were ever given those

At a farm in Butleigh two men are building up the lissoms, layers of crushed apple and straw, on the cider press. Juice is already collecting in the tub at the front.

51

names originally, I wouldn't know. By and large we know that one particular orchard will make excellent cider, another not quite so good, perhaps a little bit on the sharper side. So by using the apples from one orchard to another, which we know from experience, we can make satisfactory cider.

The flax grown by the Somerset farmers was also used within the county by a variety of craftsmen in small but essential businesses. Castle Cary, a market town, has been a centre for weaving since the Middle Ages. Thomas S. Donne, a well established flax spinner and hair seating warp manufacturer from Victorian times, took many of the local people to work in his factory. On leaving school Albert Bryant (b.1935) started working for T. S. Donne, who were then rope-makers and twine-makers of narrow fabrics.

When I first started at T. S. Donne's I had two days learning to do knots, tying the different weaver's knots, the slip knots. And from there I then went to winding the webbing in 18 yards, 36 yards, and 72 yard lengths. It was 2 inch webbing. I went right through, doing the whole process of weaving.

Rope-making in Taunton in the 1970s. The ropes are attached to hooks on the wall at the back of the ropewalk.

We made hundreds of yards for the upholstery trade, and even made webbing for undertakers for lowering the coffins in the graves. We also were making twine, string and ropes, and the last thing we were doing was making narrow tape to go around the top of slippers, all different colours, bright red, greens, blues and yellows for Marks & Spencer.

Before I started at the factory they even used to grow their own flax and dress it. The long ropewalks were interesting. We had an all-weather, inside, ropewalk which could be used if the weather was a bit inclement. When the weather was nice enough we used to be able to work outside. We used to have to take our yarns all the way down and put them on little hooks at the very bottom end. The twists were put into the different cords, ropes and twines and at a certain stage the man at the bottom waved his hand and you'd have to switch it off.

John Boyd came from Scotland in 1832 to set up a manufacturing business in horsehair in Castle Cary. In the 1950s John Boyd & Co. merged with T. S. Donne to form John Boyd Textiles. David Stickland (b.1938), an engineer and production manager of John Boyd Textiles, has worked in the textile business all his working life. The company is the only business weaving horse-hair into woven fabric and for this reason the equipment was purpose built. Some of the looms are more than one hundred years old.

The looms were cast in Bruton and were made by Boyds themselves; their men invented the looms. A Boyd's worker invented the picker machine that goes up and down and picks up one hair at a time and they've got the patent for it in the factory. Before they had the mechanised picker machines they did it by hand and they used to have children picking a single hair at a time. And then the Education Act came in and of course they stopped all that sort of thing, and so they invented the picker machine. These same picker machines are still going today with the same looms.

In proper weaving terms every time a loom does a revolution it's a 'pick', and so we've got at least a hundred hairs to the inch. So our material is very slowly made. We make three metres a day if it runs really well, because you've got a hundred hairs to the inch and our looms are only running at less than forty picks a minute, thirty-eight picks a minute.

The horse-hair is so lively. You can screw it up in your hand and it just springs back to life. It's a wonderful material.

The Mendip Hills, composed of carboniferous limestone through which water flows and emerges as springs at the foot of the hills, supply large quantities of untainted water which has

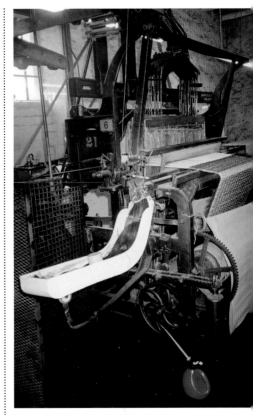

Horsehair loom at Boyds, Castle Cary. At the front of the loom is a picker machine.

allowed the development of a thriving paper-making industry. Eddie Stubbins (b.1927) was employed at St Cuthbert's Mill and Wookey Hole Mill on the edge of the Mendips. He worked in various departments making both hand-made and industrial paper.

When I started, the main ingredient for paper was esparto grass and that mainly came from South Africa and North Africa, hundreds of tons and that used to come in by boat to Bristol. It looked like straw, the same colour, but it was a rough, coarse grass and that was the main ingredient of paper in those days. We used to make all kinds of paper from Basildon Bond writing paper to paper for office uses. Different companies had their own water-marks. In the 1960s it became very competitive and we could not compete in that type of paper. At that stage esparto grass was phased out and wood pulps from all over the world took over. One of the first industrial papers that we started making was for Formica table-tops, which had to be strong and absorbent to absorb the resins that was added.

Opening bales of esparto grass from North Africa at St Cuthbert's Mill, Wookey, 1935. Sometimes snakes were found.

54

We made a lot of cheque paper for different banks and security features were built in. If you tried to forge a cheque or alter the writing on it, you'd use bleach and the whole thing would go black and discoloured. We also made bank note paper for Egypt, Thailand, and other foreign countries, mostly with rag. We made paper for maps that were used outside so it had to be strong in all winds and weathers and a chemical was added to increase its strength when it was wet.

Most villages had a cooper. In West Pennard the Hunt family were the local firm repairing and making barrels. Lionel Hunt (b.1900) worked with his father as a young man and then, in 1924, moved into the neighbouring village of Baltonsborough where he worked for Bob Clapp, the cider-maker, for many years.

Coopering ran in the family. My great-grandfather was a cooper, which must have been a hundred years before I was born.
I was what was termed a wet cooper. There are dry coopers who made casks like apple barrels, fish barrels, and things like that which did not hold liquor.
Local farmers used to bring their carts, tubs and other things to our place to be repaired. However there was another place we used to visit, Highbridge, to the wine and spirits works. This involved a train journey which meant hiring someone with a horse and trap, early morning, to take us to the station. We would then spend the whole week at Highbridge living in lodgings. Some of the barrels to be repaired were in the bonded store, others to be got ready for despatch to Scotland to be filled with whisky. This happened twice, perhaps three times, generally once in the spring and once before Christmas.
In addition, we repaired and re-made butter barrels and butter churns. These were small wooden tubs which had to be perfectly smooth with no splinters. Sandpaper was not good enough to be used on it, it had to be glazed. This meant scraping the way of the grain with a bit of broken glass which had a very keen edge and as a boy I frequently spent half a day glazing.

Maintenance of the equipment used on estates and farms relied heavily on the services of skilled village craftsmen. A wheelwright's business was a hive of activity employing carpenters, sawyers, sign writers and sometimes blacksmiths. One such business, in Brompton Regis, was run for three generations by the How family, continuing a long established tradition. Ron How (b.1910) with his two brothers Ern and Jack were the last of the family to be involved and when they retired in the early 1980s the business closed and the premises were sold.

We used to make different kinds of carts and wagons including horse-drawn cattle wagons totally enclosed. We used to do all the scribing, painting and varnishing and lettering for each individual cart. We used to have to grind our own paint when I first came here — red lead, white lead and colouring.

We made three wheeled putt carts; they used to have them out in the fields. We made milk floats to go over to Wales and curry carts with sides so you can carry hay and corn and all sorts like that. We sold wagons to firms in Basingstoke and Oxfordshire. We also made oak and elm coffins and it used to take all day to plane them up. The oak ones usually had handles of solid brass.

Ron's brother Ern (b.1916) explained how they fixed the metal rim to the wagon wheels.

The big fire was for bonding, for heating the bonds with the iron plate on top. All the bond used to be covered with the hot ash. When he was really hot then we used to turn the blower off and two come in with the tongs, you see, and carry it right out. He'd really singe the hair on your arms when he was hot.

Ron How and Miss Leadbetter, at a sale of old farm machinery, inspecting a four-wheeled flat cart made by his father, John.

Opposite page: Lionel Hunt standing on the right in his long cooper's apron.

The red hot bond being carried to the wagon wheel waiting on the bonding plate.

Pigs, sheep and markets

Pigs were kept on many farms where there was a dairy and cheese-making operation, because they could be fed whey from cheese-making. William Bartlett (b.1898) explained what else he fed his pigs on his family farm in Shepton Montague.

> Always kept about thirty sows: breed the little ones, keep them with the sow 'til two months old and pick them up and take them to market — Wincanton and Sparkford. Had markets everywhere in they days.
>
> They'd run wild, go where they liked. They do come home at night and go in a shed when we do feed them. And in the day time, specially in the fall of the year — you know what I mean, the back end of the year when the nuts would fall, and acorns — they did get off up in the woods and we didn't see them for perhaps a week. Then they'd come back eventually.
>
> When they had the young ones we had to feed them barley meal, sharps and things like that — the offal from the outside of wheat, sharps, bran. Bran is the first skin of the wheat and sharps is the next skin and the last one is the flour.

Pigs drinking at the pond in the farmyard at Moortown Farm, Curry Rivel.

Exmoor Horn sheep are found in a small area of west Somerset on the high ground of Exmoor. This area has a colder and windier climate than many other parts of the county. Sally Bassford (b.1956), from Porlock, took over the tenancy of a farm from her father and continues to breed a fine flock of sheep.

Exmoor Horn sheep are designed for this area; they live well here. We keep a base flock of pure Exmoor Horns. I've also got the cross-breds, which are a financial help, as they produce strong store lambs or prime fat lambs whereas the Exmoor Horn take a little bit longer. We do cross some with the Blue-faced Leicesters so you get your Exmoor mule ewe lambs. But the Scotch Black-face and the Swaledale crosses we primarily use on the common so we can keep our common rights going. It's called Porlock Common. It is a private common, it's not a registered common, and the farms which neighbour the common have all got a grazing right. Obviously we get hill farm allowance on it, we get an Exmoor Sensitive Area payment, so it just keeps the common alive, and I think Porlock Common is one of the best-looking commons.

Walter Baber (b.1904), from Chewton Mendip, described how they constructed and maintained the stone walls around the fields, leaving special holes to allow sheep to pass through.

> The stone was quarried on the plain often-times, right near where it was being used, to save the cartage. Often-times the foundations were gone bad, the cause of moles heaving underneath, and they'd undermine the foundations and down goes the wall eventually. So to build up the wall again, we always had to take a spade with us, sometimes a pickaxe, 'cos there were big stones for putting up on for foundations. Always, you must always insist on putting the biggest stones at the bottom and getting them level, well and truly level, then you could carry on. That's half the battle, you see. But as you build up the wall, you always want to keep the middle full, placing little small bits in under the main stones, to stop them from rocking about; we always aim to cross them all the time, not build one on top of the other — put the next one over the previous gap where the other two joined. And it was always most important, blending it into the existing, where the wall had fallen from. We always like to keep the wall straight — not to have any bellies on 'em — 'specially when you come to harvest time, you're liable to hit these bulges with the machinery, you see! But they were wonderful windbreaks as well; the cattle would lie under them during the winter months.
>
> On our farm, on the plain, there was quite a few holes built in the walls, where the shepherds used to let the sheep go through, for counting purposes. Yes. Sheep are funny things — you have far more job to get them through a gate, than through a hole in the wall; that's the way he'd use the hole, yes. Count on 'em and also check; you can look at them more as they're passing through, for their feet or maggots, or anything like that.

Market day was important for buying and selling livestock and produce. Fred Russell (b.1896), from Dundry, explained that his father was a farmer and dealer and he and his brother helped move the livestock to and from the markets, usually by road if the distance was not too far, but using the railway for longer journeys.

> The family of Burges used to come into Bristol cattle market. He would go straight to my Dad, because he was always straight in his dealings, and we were always brought up to be the same, because if you do any twisting they don't want to see you any more. On this certain Thursday he said 'Well, don't want any cattle, I could done with a few sheep'. My Dad said 'Well, I have fifty come home last night which

Walter Baber and Ann Heeley recording for the Oral Archive in February 1980.

A man driving sheep along the road to Bridgwater through Locksley Woods, on the ridge above Shapwick.

would suit you down to the ground.' It was all private dealing, see, no auctioneers, not then. They had a deal. Friday came and Father said 'Well, you had better have the old dog and take them, get them on to St. Philips and get them on the train to Yate up to Mr Burge'.

I got to St. Philips; there were three men cleaning up the cattle pens. The foreman said 'This only open Thursday's — market day — to get the cattle away from Bristol market. You'll have to take them back and bring them next Thursday.' Then I said, 'How far do you think it is from here out to Yate?' 'About ten miles.' It was about eight from us. I thought, whilst I'm here on the spot might as well take them on, get rid of them; the man will have his sheep and that will be it. Which I did. When I got within a mile of Yate a man said 'He's an old pal of mine. I'll see Mr Burge and if you are quick you'll catch a train back to Temple Meads from Yate at five o'clock'. I thanked him and he did that. I got back to Temple Meads. I had to walk along to Bedminster Bridge. I got the tramcar to Bedminster Down. I had to get out and walk back to East Dundry — three miles — and got home about seven o'clock in the evening. And when I went in, absolutely whacked out, Father said 'Well, you've been a long time! What have you been doing?'

On leaving school David Millard (b.1942) joined an established firm of auctioneers, Cooper & Tanner, as an articled clerk, and then became an auctioneer, principally of livestock. The company ran small markets such as those in Glastonbury, Frome, Shepton Mallet and Sparkford. During David's career these have all closed but a new market site near Frome has opened, which is one of the biggest in the south-west.

Glastonbury market was held on a Tuesday, and it was very largely a calf market, the biggest and certainly one of the best calf markets in the south-west of England and would have been up to eight hundred or a thousand calves.

A special market was the Christmas livestock show and sale and that was held on a normal market day, about two or three weeks in advance of Christmas. The cattle fell into two categories: what we called the haltered animals which were the ones which had halters on them and were led, and the unhaltered which were put into pens and judged. And they were done individually, the cattle. The pigs and the sheep were in groups of three or five and the calves in their various breed and sex; bulls and heifers, would have been judged individually. We always ended up with an overall champion and a reserve champion in each section and it was very much a highlight of the year.

There were two spin-offs from that fatstock show. One was the butchers used to have an open evening which they had their meat all on display, the various butchers in Glastonbury and Street, and then there was the Glastonbury Annual Fatstock Dinner which was usually about a week after the show and was one of the highlights of the year, eating-wise.

Judging the Pairs class of steers at the Christmas Fatstock Show at Glastonbury in 1957 or 1958. The judge, from Keynsham, has his hand on a steer.

CHAPTER TWO
AT HOME

IN SOMERSET IN THE EARLY twentieth century the majority of working people in the countryside lived in rented or tied accommodation, sometimes moving as the father of the household found work elsewhere. Some would spend their whole working life in one place, possibly living in one cottage. Within the farming community, farmhouses came in all sizes, but would generally have more rooms than the cottages, often including functional areas related to the type of farm. Larger houses, usually owned by wealthy landowners, were able to take advantage of modern advances. Most of the older houses in Somerset were built of local stone. During the time covered by these memories tremendous changes took place within the homes of all walks of life. Homes with mud or flagstone floors and open fires and ranges for heating and cooking, as well as oil stoves, saw the advent of electricity. Water, fetched in buckets from wells, rivers or pumps became available from a tap inside the house and with the arrival of running water and mains drainage the privy at the end of the garden was abandoned in favour of a water closet or flush lavatory. The coming of such luxuries was recalled with great clarity by men and women alike, an indication of the importance of such events.

Homes large and small

There were obvious advantages to having a good landlord. The parents of Christine Govier (b.1914) rented an estate cottage from Robert Neville Grenville, Squire of Butleigh Court estate near Glastonbury, where her father worked as a carter.

Christine Govier's first home in Water Lane, Butleigh, with bread oven on the right.

> We paid two shillings and five pence a week, that included rates, and we paid it every half year up at the Court. If you wanted anything done the Squire would provide the paint but you would have to do it yourself. And the paint was always —ooh, I don't know what colour to call it — a sort of khaki colour, always khaki brown, and for your ceilings you did get whitewash, and it used to peel off. You got an awful mess on the floors!

Gertie Tidball (b.1926), from Mark near Highbridge, was the daughter of the sexton; they were offered a cottage near the church when Gertie was seven years old. She was the youngest of four children and after marriage she and her husband continued to live with her widowed mother.

We had no water inside at all. There was a stop-tap down across the road from our gate, and we used to have to get the water in buckets and bring it in and take it into the kitchen. I'm calling it the kitchen now because these days everything is much different, because we've got kitchens and lounges and dining rooms, but we didn't have that years ago. The kitchen was called 'the back house'. That's where you did your cooking and cleaning, and we cooked with an oil stove, a three burner Florence oil stove, with an oven on the top and Mother used to cook very well with that. We had a little coal range in the other room, so sometimes you cooked on that as well. And of course, there was no electricity. We had oil lamps; we used to have

A Florence stove on display at the Blaise Castle House Museum, Bristol, similar to the one used by Gertie Tidball.

to trim the wicks and clean the globes. And candles to go to bed. We didn't have any other lights.

Mother used to make rag rugs. She used to cut up materials, different colours, dresses and things like that, cut them into rag pieces and somehow she used to twist them through, it could have been a piece of canvas. She used to make the rugs in the evenings because there was no television. She used to do darning and mending and knitting.

Inside most cottages facilities were adequate rather than comfortable, with parents and children sharing rooms and sometimes beds, achieving a degree of privacy with the use of screens. Irene Marchant (b.1935) was grateful for the screen around her bed on the upstairs landing of their cottage in Butleigh. Margery Brown (b.1919), also in Butleigh, was fortunate as she and her brother each had a small bedroom, but their widowed mother had to sleep on the draughty landing.

A rag rug in the Victorian kitchen at the Somerset Rural Life Museum, made using material from old clothes.

Margery Brown as a child sitting with her mother, Elsie Little, at their home, Whitelawns, Butleigh.

There was a very, very big landing, but there was no window there. In the bedroom that came up from the stone stairs, there was a square piece of the wall knocked away and that brought a little tiny bit of light into the landing. In the winter, when you went up over the stairs with a candle and if it was a bit draughty, it used to blow the candle out sometimes. I slept in the middle room and Ray slept in the further room and Mother slept at the top of the stairs. If you wanted to go the toilet in the winter, we didn't have torch; we had candle. And you opened the door and the candle blew out!

With living space short and families often large, neighbourliness could ease the situation. Margaret Windsor (b.1919) shared her bedroom with her four sisters, whilst her brother slept in the adjoining house.

We moved to an old farmhouse at Pilton. It was very large, very damp, and it was parted in two. We had one half and a German family, by the name of Slund, had the other half. They were a married couple with one son. My mother and father had six children; five girls and one boy. Now we had one living room and two bedrooms. Mother and father had one bedroom and we five girls had the other bedroom, which wasn't very large, and we all had to sleep in one double bed; three at the top and two at the bottom. And my mother asked Mr. Slund next door if she could put a little single bed into one of his bedrooms for my brother, which he readily agreed, and my brother slept in there.

Now in those days the toilets were always at the bottom of the garden; and so during the night we always had what you call a pot or a jeremiah. Every night when you went up to bed you opened the pedestal, took your pot out and put it under the bed. In the morning, oh dear, dear, up you went with water, a jug with some water in a pail and a cloth and you emptied the pot and you rinsed it with the water and wiped it with the cloth before you started making beds or anything else. That had to be done first. And my father always made us put it round the roses. But it was joy; the days seemed to be so long and we were so very, very happy.

Margaret Windsor, standing front left, with her family outside their cottage in Pilton in 1931.

Jim Porter (b.1932) from Butleigh, brother of Irene Marchant (b.1935), also had vivid memories of bedtime and the more practical aspects of sleeping in a house with no indoor sanitation!

I do remember we all had our beds with iron springs and we always used to have the pot underneath the bed with a large cloth over it with beads all the way around, and the reason was if you didn't put the cloth over it, it rusted the springs underneath the beds. And you could tell, when beds came up for auction, they would look at the springs, and there was always a portion where it was rusty.

Sanitation as we know it today was largely unknown, particularly in the country, until after World War II and many villages did not have mains drainage until 1960 or later. In the larger country homes water closets, for the use of the lord and lady of the house only, were installed in the nineteenth century, but houses inhabited by the less well-off remained dependent on earth closets and chamber pots well into the twentieth century.

With her six brothers and sisters Agnes Turner (b.1909), from Street, recalled queueing up at the pump for a bowl of water to throw down the toilet; Vivian Best (b.1918) coped with an outdoor toilet in the yard until she was 65 years old, when a bathroom was put into the cottage in Glastonbury where she had lived for many years; and Joyce Harris (b.1919), as a child brought up at Silver Street Farm in Congresbury, remembered having to walk through the garden to the privy.

> We had a lavatory down the bottom of the garden and a wooden seat, you know, and there was a big lawn and a shrubbery at the bottom of this lawn, and you'd go down the path to the lavatory. It was concealed with this shrubbery. Each of us

Far left: *Pump outside the back door of Church Farm, Shapwick, 1987.*

Left: *Outside privy at Keeper's Cottage, Butleigh, in 1978.*

had to take turns to scrub the lavatory on a Saturday. Well, we didn't like doing that, but we didn't like doing anything really. It was just that we had our allotted tasks so it didn't hurt us really, when you look back. We were all occupied with something, you know, some job or other.

As late as 1950 Margaret Brown (b.1924) and her new husband took a cottage in Cannington that still had very basic facilities with no running water but there was an electrical supply.

I became pregnant and so we looked for somewhere to be on our own and we found a tiny cottage, three or four hundred years old, with a mud floor, which my husband asked the landlord, could he have it concreted, and the landlord gave permission. So he had that done before we went in. And one living room, one bedroom, a tiny scullery, water outside, and the lavatory at the top of the garden.

We shared the water outside, which was a pump, and there was a shed with a copper that we were supposed to share, but my husband's godmother died and left him £100 and he bought himself a dinner jacket and me a washing machine, which was absolutely wonderful! So I would have to get the water in from outside, heat it up on the electric stove, put it in the washing machine and when I had enough it would do the washing.

Pump outside the back door of Henley Farm, Henley, 2009.

Margaret Brown beside her Rayburn.

Gloria McClurg (b.1941) had early experiences of the conditions at Turnbridge Cottage where she and her parents and grandparents lived in Meare, near Glastonbury.

We lived in a cottage which belonged to my grandfather. It didn't have any amenities at all; we had no drainage, no running water, and no electricity. My father used to go to my uncle's farm and fill a churn of water and we had three churns of water a week. That was just drinking water. For washing and washing clothes, we had to get water out of the water barrel from outside, the rainwater that had been collected. We had a neighbour who had a huge water barrel; if ours ran dry or got a bit mucky, we actually got some from there. On occasions, my father and I have gone up to the river bridge at Turnbridge and actually dipped buckets into the river to get water out when it was clear.

We just had a bucket toilet which had to be emptied and you had to go along the river bank and it wasn't very nice in the wintertime.

Gloria McClurg in 2007.

Stone slab in the back kitchen of a cottage in Butleigh.

The family moved into a new council house in the same village in 1959.

It was a complete change of life: it made life much easier for my mother. It was a bit bigger and of course it had all modern things like electricity, water, drainage. In fact, it had two toilets; one downstairs and one upstairs and that was a luxury to us. The new council house was amazing. I went round just switching lights on and off because it was just a novelty, you know, to be able to just do that! We were very careful with our water and things because we'd been so careful before with our water that to start off with, it was a bit strange to have all this extra stuff that we didn't have before.

Obviously mother was still doing all the cooking and cleaning. Now she had a Rayburn to cook on, and as well as that a small electric stove that they bought second-hand. We had an electric kettle!

We had a pantry in the new house and it had a stone slab that we kept things cool on. And in the summer, my mum always had a bucket with the milk bottles sitting in to keep them cool. So we didn't have a 'fridge for quite a while and I suppose she got so used to not having these things that she didn't really need them all straight away.

We had just the kitchen and a living room. That was the only two rooms downstairs. Most things went on in the kitchen — cooking, eating, ironing, everything she had to do in that one room — and the living room was kept for relaxing in the evenings, round the radio.

The elderly without families to care for them could be allocated accommodation in an almshouse. In Lympsham an unknown benefactor had built a row of cottages, in South Road, near South Farm where Joan Claydon (b.1932) lived with her parents.

Just beyond South Farm were the almshouses. There were two rooms, one up, one down, with a fairly substantial wooden ladder going between the two — the up and down room. The rent was something like sixpence. I don't know whether it was sixpence a week or sixpence a month, but they were for the poorer families of the village, and they were always known as the poor-houses. If father was sawing logs or something, he would always give some to them for their fires, you see, and he always said, 'If you give to one you've got to give to them all,' because otherwise they were very jealous of one having something without the other. I think it was mainly women and my mother used to keep an eye on them and if they were ill she'd always take them a little egg custard. And there was a marvellous occasion when she took an egg custard to one dear old lady called Mrs Poole, and the day after she took the egg custard Mrs Poole died. And her daughter came along to Mother and she said, 'Oh, Mrs Cook, thank you very much for bringing that little custard to Mother. She did enjoy it and she's died.' And my mother was never allowed to forget this as you can imagine!

South Farm, a farmhouse built in 1869, was substantial compared to the majority of the homes in the village although the basic facilities varied little. It was large enough to be able to accommodate paying guests to supplement the farm income. One family who came each year was the Reverend John G. Derrick and his wife and three children, and it is as a result of his

Almshouses in Lympsham, close to South Farm.

South Farm, Lympsham, c.1900, home of Joan Claydon.

hobby of photography that we can see the exteriors of both South Farm and the almshouses at the end of the nineteenth century. Joan remembered the inside of South Farm.

It had a front door with a nice porch with roses round it and then you went into a small entrance hall and there was a room on either side. You went into the dining room and through into what we originally called the kitchen. There was a large walk-in pantry and you went through to the back entrance of the house where there was a lean-to with a sink and cold water tap and a copper boiler, and leading from there was what we always called the wash-house which was where the washing was done. Stone-floored, of course, very cold, so there was a big meat-safe in there, and the milk that one was using in the house was always kept there and anything that needed to be kept cool.

The stairs went up from the front hall quite steeply, and upstairs there were four bedrooms. The two at the front had fireplaces in them which I can remember, when

I wasn't well, fires being lit in those. No bathroom, of course; an outside loo round the back of the house. It was a flush loo in my day but of course before that it had been an earth closet, obviously. But no bathroom until, I think it was after the war, when one of the bedrooms was then converted into a bathroom.

Landlords sometimes recorded their ownership of property visibly. In Butleigh nameplates with GNG or RNG mark the cottages and farmhouses renovated by George Neville Grenville or his son Ralph. In North Curry the initials WB for William Barrett were found on farm buildings and gates, fondly remembered by local inhabitants Bill Board and Hilda Denman.

In an estate village with a resident Squire, the house itself was a place of work for domestic servants and their memories reflected the nature of their employment. In his account of his duties at Butleigh Court, John Axford (b.1910), footman and later butler, mentioned a whole series of rooms he used for specific purposes: servants' hall, kitchen, pantry, game larder, bake house, meat larder, milk larder, housekeeper's room; and others for the use of the Squire and his family – morning room, dining room, bedrooms, drawing room, hall and library. Muriel Lovering (b.1913) worked as a second housemaid in Butleigh Court from 1930 until Robert Neville Grenville died in 1936. The account of her duties gives a picture of the size and grandeur of the accommodation.

Indoor staff at Butleigh Court, on the occasion of John Axford's 21st birthday, July 27th 1931. He is on the right, with Muriel Lovering standing third from the left.

Well, first thing in the morning our first duty was to get the kettle boiling for to make Mrs Neville Grenville a cup of tea and take it through the hall to the dressing room for the lady's maid to give her, six-thirty in the morning. And then we, the two under-housemaids, had six fireplaces to do and the rooms before our breakfast at eight. We had to sweep, push Ewbanks like, and mop the floorboards round and all the dusting but the head housemaid, she dusted what we called the levels; what she could do standing, you see. The under-housemaid had to do all the skirtings, all the things that was low, and I had to do all what we called the tops which was the higher things because we all had to work together to get it done in the time.

Then we had breakfast at eight o'clock and then we had to do the servants' bedrooms until we were ready for prayers at nine o'clock in the dining room. It was led in with the lady's maid, housekeeper, the head housemaid, then I was there and Bet Durston the under housemaid. Then was the cook, the kitchen maid and the scullery maid followed by the butler, footman and hallboy. And after prayers, we each had to go to do our different work which was listed for the month. I had to do everything thoroughly once a month which included the dining room, the

Staff at Butleigh Court holding the tools of their trade; Muriel Lovering is second from the left, with John Axford on the far right.

saloon, the library, the hall, the lady's maid's room and the morning room which Mrs Grenville used as her private room, and the secretary's room, me keeping all the spare bedrooms clean. A lot of the rooms were scrubbed boards, but the best landing had a carpet down and scrubbed boards either side. We did all the brass one day and all the stone steps on another day. We had a day which we did stone steps like and then we had a day for the spare rooms which are named.

There was the Oak Room in which we kept all the best linen and how I remember it so well, I had to open that door every morning and at the side there was the measurements of what water there was in the tank which supplied the Court. It was like in an old grandfather's clock, with two cords. Well, you pushed one of those cords up with the weight on and then let it gradually come down, and how much water was in the tank was measured on a side slab. I had to give the Squire the number every day.

There was a small passage and up a flight of stairs was the room called the Thackeray Room, where all the vestments for the church were kept in a massive chest of drawers. Each week I had to put one lot away and bring down whichever Mrs Grenville said we needed. Also in that room I can remember we always dried all the lavender for the lavender bags that were made for our use and for the bazaars.

Water heating, washday and baths

Heating for a large house, and provision of hot water, would not have been easy. At Butleigh Court the servants carried cans of water to supply the wash stands and hip baths. Donald Phillips' (b.1927) mother was brought up in Moredon House, a substantial country house in North Curry, where they had memorable bathrooms. Two huge baths with duck boards at the side had been put into a room with a dividing partition between them. This partition did not reach to the ceiling which provided much fun for the children bathing either side, armed with wet sponges!

The home that Margaret Windsor (b.1919) moved into in Pilton had no bathroom when she was growing up, so the back kitchen was used by the family for bathing.

> We used to have a bath in one of these oval-shaped baths and we always had to heat the water in the old fashioned copper, and to heat the water we used to burn newspapers, old shoes, any old rags, anything to heat the water, because coal, although it was very cheap, wasn't cheap because you didn't have the wages in those days. And then my father and my brother would be sent out and we four girls would have a bath in the same water in front of the one and only fireplace.
> And when I was about fifteen or sixteen we had what they called the 'Bungalow bath'; it was about four foot long and you could stretch your legs out. Well then, when you got to that age it was time to have a bath in the back kitchen and the only heat you had was the little bit of heat from the fire under the copper. In fact our back kitchen was half underground so you can guess how cold it was in there. The

Susan Ellen Anning collecting firewood from a wood pile outside her back door.

Bungalow bath on display at the Blaise Castle House Museum, Bristol.

bolt was outside not inside, so when you had a bath someone would lock the door. Now the larder was on one end of this long narrow back kitchen, and one Saturday afternoon, I suppose I was seventeen, and I was there sat in this bath and the bolt shot back and who walked in but the butcher! Can you imagine it! I couldn't stand up, I couldn't do anything. But he said 'Hello, Margo'. And he walked straight in, he put the meat in the larder — and in those days we had a cover that went over to keep the flies off of it because there were no fridges, no electricity — and he put this thing over the meat, shut the larder door, said 'Cheerio, Margo', locked the door and that was that. I felt dreadful. You think of being seventeen, and having the butcher walk in when you were in the bath!

For all householders not only was it hard work to make sure there was sufficient water in the house for its many uses, but it also then had to be heated for laundry and bathing. This was achieved using a variety of methods: open fires in the kitchen fuelled with hand-bound faggots of wood, logs, peat or coal; or a furnace, sometimes known as a boiler, in the back kitchen or an outhouse.

Having lived there since he was a boy, Ernest Pearce (b.1907) took over the tenancy from his father on a farm in Fiddington in 1945. He remembered how his mother heated the water.

Hearth oven with a bundle of faggots at a farm in Hardington Mandeville in 1985.

> Mother used to burn the faggots in the house to heat the water and the baths for us. We had no hot water system, so she used to heat the water in the back kitchen on the branders with the saucepans and these faggots — you just put a whole faggot in. Faggots are sticks you cut about three foot long and you tie a binder round them, that's a faggot.
> She put a whole faggot in underneath and when it burned in the middle she used to push the ends in from each side and then when that was gone she'd put on another one. We used to have a big faggot rick outside the house, you see. Every year we laid the hedges and made the faggots for the winter fuel. There was no oil in those days for to heat the house.

On the family farm in Spaxton, Tom Merchant (b.1914) remembered vividly the use of faggots for cooking as well as heating water, and the subsequent disposal of the large amount of ashes that resulted and how those were put to good use.

Tom and Nancy Merchant of Fiddington in 1983.

> Every day you'd have two great big bucketfuls of wood ash, and there in the yard was a shed — oh, I suppose it would be about twelve foot square! — with a big arch where we used to throw the ashes in, and he'd fill up with ashes during the winter

Crocks hanging over an open fire at a farm in Ashbrittle.

months, and then in the spring we used to have the horses and putts, and back in, and throw the ashes into the carts, and take it out and put it on the land for swedes. There was a lot of potash; that was good stuff.

Joyce Harris (b.1919) had memories of helping her mother on washday at home in Congresbury. The water used for washing from the well in the garden was carried by buckets. In the afternoon after the big wash, the hot soapy water was used to scrub all the stone floors.

We had one of these old furnaces. We'd light the fire underneath. It was a big round one, and we used to put the washing in there and boil it; the sheets and the pillow cases, all the white stuff; used to have a big rod to fish it out with.
It then went into a great big galvanised bath, but we did have a big wooden bath as well that we used to use for the washing, I remember. We used to have one of those old-fashioned things you rub the washing on, metal sort of things. We used to rub the very heavy stuff on that, but it was mostly the shirts and things like that they used to soak. They didn't used to wash trousers because the material would shrink,

but they used to get quite sort of dirty.

We had to put the baths up on a bench: we didn't have sinks but we had to put them on benches to not to be bending over. You would stand up and do it, and rub without getting the back ache.

My mother used to buy a great big bar of soap. She could buy it in a box of about 12 pound in weight, all these big, long things, bars of soap, and then we'd cut off what we needed. That would be kept and that was very economical because the longer you kept it, the harder it was. We used to grate up the soap to soak the washing in. We didn't have soap powders. We had to be very fussy about rinsing. We had a lovely well in the garden so we had heaps of water.

We'd have a great big bowl and heave the washing out into this and then put it into the bath for swilling, and we used to have to swill it about three times and then put it through the mangle to get the surplus water out. We did wring the thinner things but most of it went through the mangle. Of course you could set it, you know, and

Poster advertising Sunlight soap, showing hand-washing clothes in a wooden tub.

79

Mangle in the courtyard at the Somerset Rural Life Museum, used for demonstrations.

the wood used to wear out, and eventually there was a little gap where over the years it had got a bit worn in the middle.

The flat irons were heated on top of the range. You heat them, you see. You keep having to change them because they wouldn't stay hot very long. We had a great big wooden kitchen table. We had big blankets to start with and then have a sheet— that was our padding for the ironing.

My mother used to have a valance, lovely white cotton with a lace inset to it, that was stitched on to the base of the bed. And then they had what you call a goffering iron which would make little ridges to go round the bottom, like curling tongs that would make the edge look attractive. These would have to be put inside the range, because they couldn't go on the top.

It is very apparent that from a very early age the children, particularly the girls, were involved with washing day. Grace Parish (b. 1919) in Pawlett on a farm, related how her mother had help with her washing but when the lady gave up Grace was informed that washday would be moved from Monday to Saturdays when she was at home.

I was only about eleven and I used to first of all make the Robins starch. It was one tablespoon of starch to two tablespoons of cold water and you mixed that to a paste and then you poured boiling water on it and you kept pouring until you had the right consistency to dip the tablecloths and shirt collars and all sorts of things. So that was my first job and then I had to turn the wringer for my mother, she used to put everything through the wringer twice because in those days the clothes took so much longer to dry. It was all pure cotton and pure wool. And then I had to peg out; I put all the washing on the line. So that is how I spent my Saturdays!

Olive Stone (b.1897) had memories of the method of cleaning flat irons with scrapings of dust from a yellow brick and Margaret Windsor's (b.1919) family rubbed a bar of soap on the dirty iron and then polished it vigorously on a cloth spread on the ironing table.

Esther Venn (b.1922) lived at Kilton Farm, Kilton, until she was nine, when her father moved to Thurloxton. Esther had memories of help with the family washday.

The washing was done by a marvellous lady who came on Monday morning and in the scullery was a big copper and it was a copper copper. It wasn't an iron copper. It was a beautiful one. In fact when it was stopped being used I took it out and polished it up and had it in the drawing room for logs, and very handsome it was.

Washing on the line outside a cottage in Porlock Weir.

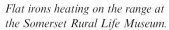

Flat irons heating on the range at the Somerset Rural Life Museum.

Nell Stuckey hanging out washing at Yew Tree Farm, Kingston Seymour.

Dorothy Rendell as a young woman.

Pattens on display at the Somerset Rural Life Museum.

And that would be filled with soft rain water and the fire would be lit underneath and all the clothes would go in and be boiled. And then she'd take it out into a big galvanized tub and rub-a-dub-dub and into a great wooden receptacle, with a mangle on the end, and go out on the line. And it was lovely when it came in, all smelling of sweet, sweet summer air, it was delightful. Not so good in the winter when it was frozen stiff!

Dorothy Rendell (b.1906) in East Coker, remembered as a young child visiting Aunt Lizzie in West Coker who ran a laundry, taking in washing from the large houses in the district.

She had a great big shed in the orchard where all the women used to do the laundry. And there were all these tubs of laundry and boards to rub the washing on because there was no laundry machines then. There was scrubbing brushes and all sorts of things. It was full of steam and there were women scrubbing away. There was a big orchard and there were lines between the trees and they used to hang the washing out there and then the women used to iron it all.
And Aunt Lizzie had a donkey cart and she used to pile these great big laundry baskets in the back of the donkey cart and go round and deliver them. It used to take two people to put the baskets on the thing and sometimes her husband went with her. He was a nice little man, but he was as small as she was big. She was a great big person. But ever so jolly, always laughing. Never heard her grumble about anything. Every time we went, no matter what time of the day it was, there was a great big saucepan of potatoes on the open fire. And there was always cold meat and a great big dish of potatoes for all the women to eat for their lunch.

Nancy Wallis (b.1903) recalled the atmosphere in the back kitchen and laundry in her home at the Rectory in Fitzhead, where she could see nothing but thick steam and the faces of the old washerwomen who came once a fortnight, and whose feet shod with pattens made distinctive marks in the mud leading to the washing line in the garden.

Kitchens and cooking

In all homes the kitchen was the most important room, not only for cooking and preparing food, but also as the one room with constant heat from open hearth fires or a cast iron solid fuel range.

Maurice Symes (b.1896) talked about his grandmother's cooking arrangements at Pattens Farm, Coat, in the early twentieth century, which was also his home all his working life.

*The Rendell family c.1909.
Dorothy is sitting on her
mother's knee.*

Sparks fly when using a faggot to light the hearth fire at Dairy House Farm, Hardington Mandeville.

They had a steel hearth fire with a steel back to it, and under the fire was a hearth oven. It was the whole width of the fireplace with an oven under the fire with a door and shelves just like an ordinary oven. And then there was a little trap door and another fire under this hearth oven. Then in addition to that there was this bread oven. That was built into the wall like a baker's oven; they did their own baking in the kitchen.

Most of the cooking was done over the open fire. They used to have adjustable hooks that you can move up and down, and a contraption, which she always called a brandis, that you hooked on to put saucepans on. You put two or three saucepans on there. Or if you only wanted the kettle, you just put the kettle onto the hooks. The chimney part was almost the width of the room, and on each side you would probably find two or three hams hanging up in bags with salt. They would be kept there in smoke from the fire up in the chimney. They seemed to stop there indefinitely. There seemed to be always a ham up there at any time of the year.

Every farmer's wife knew how to make bread, and would make a large supply at a time, sometimes with families getting together for the occasion. However, those without bread ovens would buy from the village baker.

In Compton Dundon Joe Witcombe (b.1897) remembered, as a child, his mother making bread in her wooden washtub.

Father always grew an acre of wheat, best wheat, and he would keep that special to thrash, to grind for bread. Mother had a big oven, back in the corner of the kitchen, and many, many a batch of bread I've helped my poor old mother put in that oven, when I was a boy. We would go to Street for two or three pennyworth of yeast. She would have her washing tub, fill him half full of flour. She knew exactly what to put in there. And a kettle of nice warm, lukewarm, water and put in her yeast and what she called 'lay the leaven'.

And next morning when she'd done her work and come to it, she would push all this in and mix it all up, the dough, and put it up on her kitchen table, and do it up in cakes, about handfuls, work it about nice and clean and lay them back in the tub. She'd have about a dozen of them or more and she'd put them in that tub and cover with her clean table-cloth and they'd all rise again. She'd get one of us to lift it up on the table again; she'd clean the tub out and put it in a big heap.

This was when it was ready for the oven, but before that we boys, I especially, would bring in a faggot of sticks and light the fire in the oven. Heat him up, put in some

good sticks, no coal, all sticks, and we used to put it in there and she used to look in and it would generally take an hour, an hour and a half, then wait till it had burnt down like a fire would, and then she had a curled iron crook, and we used to hook out the ashes and get it all clean.

And when she was ready, the word 'go!' Up goes the dough on the table and she'd cut out in loaves, she'd cut out a nice fair piece, put down on the table like that and she'd cut out another smaller piece and put on the top and she had her knuckles and put in the top and just give them a twist like that and that was that little hole in the top of the loaf. And then she had a pile — a wooden shovel — put him up on the table, and have a bit of flour and sprinkle all over the pile, and put him ready for Mother to put her first loaf and then the second like that, and when she had

The Witcombe family at the Old Rectory Farm in Compton Dundon; Joe is standing on the left.

him ready she'd grab the pile from you and pop back and shovel him right to the back of the oven.

She used to bake seven loaves, seven pound each, roughly. Brown loaves. And then she used to cook a joint of meat, a rabbit or a fowl or a small loaf, up round the front that would come out first. Then the big loaves had to go back one hour longer and they would come out perfect and that was one loaf a day, one seven pound loaf —never buy no bread. Never buy no potatoes, never buy much meat. She did practically keep ourselves, and she did that in addition to everything else she was expected to do – wonderful!

Elizabeth Tincknell (b.1904) and her sister Minnie Vowles (b.1905) recalled their early home life in Mudgley. Their father was a hedger and ditcher, earning about two shillings a day when they were children. Their diet consisted mainly of fruit and vegetables, especially potatoes which their father grew, not only around their cottage but also out on the moor. They did not have a lot of meat, a little lamb, but mostly just the fowls their mother kept for supplying the family with eggs.

Potato patch in the vegetable garden of Henley Cottage, Butleigh, 1976.

Phyllis Jones (b.1918) from Burrowbridge, remembered her mother and grandmother baking for the two farming families. They would bake on a Tuesday using a hundredweight of flour and two huge saucepans of cooked potatoes, to make better bread; and also dough cakes. The nearby River Parrett was a useful source of slime to seal the bread oven doors once the bread was inside, and it was also a source of free fish for the family in the spring when the elvers went down the river in great numbers on their way to the sea.

The elver time was a great time along the River Parrett. They used to get Mother to go into Hoopers of Bridgwater to get the old canvas net and she used to sew it onto this big net affair with a long handle. And they would go down along in the spring; they come up with the tides, but if it was cold they wouldn't.
We used to bring them in and they were all frothing and all scooping about, and they put them in the bucket and they poured boiling water on to scald them. They would be grey when you picked them up, but when you scalded them, they would be white. Then you washed them four or five times to get all the froth out of them, and then you put them in a little bit of salt water and leave them all night.

Two men catching eels on the River Parrett at Burrowbridge.

Elvers being collected in a bucket.

Singeing the hairs off the pig in preparation for butchering.

You washed them again and then you drained them and then you put them in a frying pan with a drop of water and just cooked them lightly. You drain off the water and then you put a little bit of fat and beat up three or four eggs and cook them all in, and then you put a plate on top and let them brown like bubble and squeak, and they are gorgeous. You cut them out like a cake. We'd eat that at supper time, generally, supper time, or else sometimes I've known Mother cook them at breakfast if the men wanted them.

Rook shooting parties were regular events in villages, as William Say (b.1919), of Butleigh, recalled. The boys used to pick the rooks up after they had been shot and he remembered the lice from the rooks running all over them. The boys were given half a dozen rooks each which they took home to be cooked and eaten.

When the shoot was over and it was getting dumpsy dark they used to give us half-a-dozen young rooks each. We used to take them home and that was actually a marvellous feast. Used to put them in boiling water to get all the feathers off and then clean them, get their insides out, then skin them and make a rook pie with the legs and the breast and the wings. Honest to God, I can taste that now. It was absolutely beautiful.

For many families keeping a pig was an important part of their diet. Maurice Symes (b.1896), of Coat, described the killing and curing of a pig for his family.

When we were getting short of meat, we would kill a pig and the travelling butcher would come round with his basket and his knives, and there were no humane killers or anything in those days. You just put them on a pig's horse, cut their throats, and that was the end of the pig. But then they had practically boiling water poured all over them and scraped all the hair. They had like old candlesticks, sharpened up and they scraped and scraped and get all the hair off. We had those big leads about five feet long and the butcher would come and cut it all up in joints and it would be put in these leads. I wonder we didn't all die of lead poisoning really. Mother would rub salt into them every morning for a couple of weeks perhaps, morning after morning, and would then drain off the liquid. There was always an outlet in these leads to let the liquid drain off and then she would go all through the process again. And it would simply stay there until we wanted it. There was no fridge or anything in those days.

In many households it was necessary to make small quantities stretch to feed a family. Margaret Windsor (b.1919) in North Wootton remembered the meals her mother used to prepare.

We only had an egg on Sundays. My mother used to boil an egg and she used to say, 'I have got a treat for you today, half an egg each.' She is the only woman I know who put an egg on the table, take a large carving knife and slice that egg in half, and pick up both halves without spilling any of the yolk! I can remember I have had as many as four slices of bread with half an egg, and every bit of that bread had one spot of yolk on it, but it used to taste beautiful. We also went through patches where you could have bread and butter or bread and jam with no butter. But it was the sign of the times: I mean everyone was the same. We were no different to all the other families in the village. If it hadn't been for the poor old rabbit, half the time, we would have gone very, very hungry. I've had roast rabbit, and I have had rabbit pie, rabbit stew, and in fact I had a rabbit last week and thoroughly enjoyed it.

Laying hens in nest boxes at Bradwell Farm, Westport, 2008.

A Herald range, similar to the one used by Grace Parish.

She used to buy six pennyworth of bones and the day she cooked the bones we would have the meat off the bones and then she would make soup with the rest. She always kept a stock pot. Ever since I can remember my mother had an oval-shaped iron crock which she always had stock in. There was a great hook coming down the chimney and this crock was always on this hook. And when we used to come home from school in the afternoon, if it was very cold, she would say, 'There's soup in the saucepan, children.' We could always go to that saucepan and have a cup of hot soup.

And I used to have to pick up the ashes and make the beds before I went to school. And when I used to be picking up the ashes she used to tell me all about cooking. And she used to say 'Now, if you want to make a good soup you must have pearl barley.' I can to this day, whenever I have anything to do with a fireplace, I can hear my mother saying, 'Now, if you want to make a good soup you must have pearl barley.'

Grace Parish (b.1919) moved as a two year old from Berrow to Pawlett with her parents. Grace talked about methods of cooking used by her mother and grandmother.

They had a fire on the hearth at one time and then they installed an iron range. I remember it was a Herald range and you had the oven at one side, and the fire at the other side. When you wanted to do a lot of cooking you could fold a canopy down and make a hob and the fire would go over the top of the oven and up the flue that way. But if you were not cooking and wanted to sit beside the fire, then you could open up a canopy, and you had a fire you could see.

But I can remember my grandmother having what you call a Dutch oven. You see, she did not have a proper oven that would heat up to cook meat, so she had a tripod that had a basting tray and a canopy that came up around, so that when she put the meat on a skewer, it faced the fire. It was open to the fire but the canopy behind kept the cold air from the meat; and she would turn it every so often.

We always had a joint, I suppose. Sunday it was roasted, Monday it was cold, Tuesday it was jugged, or a cottage pie or a stew or something. Of course, we were at school at this time and we took sandwiches for our lunch, then when we came home dinner was always put back for us. She would cook quite a bit, you see, at mid-day and the dinner was put into two basins on top of saucepans of water and put on the stove, and it was kept hot and when we came in from school we had our cooked meal. We always had a cooked meal every day.

Mum used to make cakes by rubbing the fat into the flour. It was currant cakes and things like that and it was not until I went to some cookery classes and I learnt to cream the butter and sugar that we made the cakes the way they make them now. We always had plenty of fruit. There was an orchard and apples were picked and stored, and we had apple pie, apple dumplings, stewed apple, apple sauce. And then in its turn we had rhubarb in the spring and then gooseberries, then the plums. She always made jam. She made plenty of blackcurrant jam, because we used to shoot quite a few hares on the farm and we always had a jugged hare with blackcurrant jam.

Margaret Shreeve (b.1939) is the daughter of Bob and Frances Mapstone who farmed at Abbey Farm, Glastonbury, now the Somerset Rural Life Museum. Margaret remembered the meals cooked by her mother.

We always helped with the washing up but Mother basically did all the cooking and I suppose I must have helped a bit with preparing vegetables. We had the two big vegetable gardens, so all our vegetables were home-grown, and, yes, she was a very plain cook but a very good cook. My father always had a big breakfast, he always had to have his fried egg and bacon, and fried bread.

And then lunches were always a big lunch; we called it dinner in those days. It was always meat and two veg and then a pudding, which was very often fruit pie because we had lots of fruit, and cream of course, from the dairy. Mother scalded the cream to get it to keep. And then we always had high tea, and that would be something on toast maybe or in season we'd have seakale with a cheese sauce or cauliflower with cheese sauce or Spam. I seem to remember quite a lot of Spam. And salad, of course, we grew in the summer, and she grew tomatoes, and cucumbers and marrow. And then my father would have supper at some ungodly hour, which was cheese and biscuits and pickles, and he used to have beer to drink. And in the early days we had our barrels in the cellar full of cider, and I'd be sent down with a pint mug to fetch a pint of cider to go with the meal.

A well-stocked vegetable patch in a cottage garden in Compton Street, Butleigh.

Gladys Withers (b.1900) in Babcary recalled a suet, apple, cinnamon and fresh cider pudding which her mother made in a big iron pot bubbling on the hob all day, the most delicious pudding in the world. She also described the medicinal uses of cider.

If we had colds as children, some cider would be heated and root ginger grated into it, and brown sugar or golden syrup or honey put in to make a beverage, and we would drink it as hot as we could, just a little glass. It was a sure cure for a cold! And my father, if he had a cold, he would have some toast made and it must be burnt black, and cut up in cubes and put in a basin, and this hot cider lashed with

Gladys Withers in 1983.

the ginger, and oh, quite a sizeable glass of whisky and brown sugar. And he would eat that, and drink what was left afterwards, and that was a very good cure for colds, supposed to be.

But my father once had an illness; it was gout. Before the doctor came, one of my father's employees came in to see him to talk over something to do with the business, and he said, 'Ah boss, I be sorry ye'll be like this, but I tell 'ee what 'tis, Sir. 'Tis that there cider, 'tis all the acid, see, that don't do 'ee no good. I bet that's what 'tis'. So the next day the doctor came and my father said, 'Doctor, do you think drinking cider has brought on this attack of gout?' The doctor was not a talkative man but he smiled to himself and went on counting out pills which he gave to my father and said, with a very smug look on his face, 'Now be careful to take these regularly and wash them down with some of your best quality cider!'

The health of the family was often reliant on traditional remedies. Agnes Turner (b.1909) of Street, spoke about her mother who was a nurse, and the care she took with her children.

Mother didn't believe in vaccination. She always made spring medicines for us and we always had cod liver oil. We never had much wrong with us all. She used to have

Agnes Turner, in the centre of the middle row, with her brothers and sisters.

92

a big basin and she used to have sulphur, lemons, Epsom salts and a little castor oil and we used to have to take that once a week in the spring. But it was always on a weekend during the holidays and we were never allowed out over the weekend. We all had to take that and she was always there on hand to watch over us, you know. And we never had any skin trouble whatsoever; we all had very nice skin. We always used carbolic soap. She was very particular, was mother.

The arrival of electricity

One of the greatest improvements in the life of women in any household was the installation of electricity. It arrived at different times in the villages, but for those who remembered life without it, their memories were very vivid. What a difference electric light made to homes. Refrigerators, vacuum cleaners, electric irons and washing machines for the clothes also became available and relieved the women of much drudgery. Electrically operated water pumping stations brought water into the houses at the turn of a tap.

Esther Venn of Thurloxton, August 2005.

Farmer's daughter Esther Venn (b.1922) was living on the Portman estate at Thurloxton when electricity for lighting only was put in by the landlord, who paid half the cost. It was completed just before war broke out.

We didn't have electricity until 1939. Oh, the excitement of having electricity! We were so thrilled because it was touch and go. We had a firm from Taunton who wired us, Mr West, and was it going to be done in time before we knew war was going to break out? You could feel it coming nearer and nearer and, you know, shall we get there in time? It was almost more important than the war with the electric, and we just got there in time!

Joy Vigar (b.1928) and her parents had no electricity at Manor Farm, High Ham, until she was in her twenties.

Tin advert for Royal Daylight Oil in the Somerset Rural Life Museum.

We had no electricity until 1951 and the main water came through the village at the same time. The booster, which is on the way to Langport, was manned by electricity so until the electricity came through the water couldn't get to us.
Well, it meant that instead of going to bed with candles that you put on a switch and went to bed like that. And I think the first thing that my mother bought was a cleaner. You slowly bought things to use. Before electricity Mother kept her food down the well. Butter and things like that in a bucket on a rope.

Stanley Cook on a Ferguson tractor in the late 1940s, at South Farm, Lympsham.

The cost of installing electricity was a great deterrent to many people. For Marion Brown (b.1911) of Westhay and her recently widowed mother, struggling to get a Tuberculin Testing (TT) Licence to produce milk, it was another worrying expense only mitigated by another family member stepping in to lend them the money.

> Me and my mother, we were very dubious about it because you see it all happened together. There was my father's funeral expenses to be paid for, and they were bringing the electric out. I had to have a milk house because they said they wouldn't let mother have a TT licence without a proper milk house. 'Well,' Mother said, 'we shall never be able to afford it all.' I said, 'No, Mother', and she said, 'Well, what a nuisance — only got about three or four cows and won't let us carry on the same without a milk house.' Either we sell the cows or have a milk house. So my cousin came down. 'I tell you what, Marion', he said, 'If you want the electric, while 'tis going through the moor here, you have it', he said, 'and I'll lend you the money.' 'Well', I said, 'that's very kind of you', and then he said, 'You can pay me back a bit at a time.' So that's how we had the electric.

Although Lionel Wilcox (b.1919) remembered with pride that he was the one of the first few to have access to generated electricity in the village of Stogursey after the war, it had its limitations. His sister Daphne, living in a part of the village still without this new vital resource, used to go to her mother's house to watch television.

I went back to the local garage when I came out of the Forces and they were the only place in the village that had electricity. They made their own, of course, and I lived in the house next door and I was the only one with electricity in the village because that belonged to the garage. The only trouble was when they stopped the engine at nine o'clock in the evening I had no lights! And they had no storage, so I converted back to oil lamps after nine o'clock at night.

Some people found their own solutions to the problem of getting electricity into the house. Hugh Flatt (b.1917) was an early advocate of organic farming, running his mixed farm at Huish Champflower according to strict principles. They had no electricity until 1961, when he installed a wind generator to give them their own limited supply.

We had a basic farmhouse. Our loo was in the garden. I felt it was important for farmers to have gardens and I used to compost the waste from our loo, and put it back on the garden, and we grew very good garden crops. We were not on the electricity, and in 1961 we put up a wind generator because there was plenty of wind on the Brendons, and this produced light. At first it was very spasmodic because the wind didn't blow all the time, and I bought a large number of accumulator type batteries from an operating theatre that was closing down, and kept them for emergency kit. So when the wind was blowing in the daytime it put our batteries right for the night time; but it only gave us light, it didn't give us power.

Early electric light in a kitchen at Milborne Port.

Chitcombe Farm near Huish Champflower on the Brendon hills where Hugh Flatt installed a wind generator to provide energy for lighting.

Butleigh churchyard, 1978.

Opposite page:
The three children of Bob Cotton of Manor Farm, Coxbridge, Glastonbury, playing with their toys under the supervision of two maids.

Family occasions

Phyllis Jones (b.1918) from Hales Farm, Burrowbridge, recalled, when young, the events following a death and the preparations for the funeral undertaken by the household.

There was women about the villages that would do nothing else but prepare for funerals, this is what they used to do. There was three women in our village used to do all this, and used to come and lay the people out when they died.

At a funeral everybody had to be in black, even their hankies were white edged with black or with black stripes, and white shirts. The men had a black bowler, and most of the women had black veils. They would go to the funeral, but the women had to get a terrific meal ready for them when they come back, and they would have the house full of relatives, every relative whatever you heard of was dug up and would come to the funeral. I never remember going to a funeral, we all had to stay home. But we were put in black as well, and all the blinds was drawn until the corpse was buried. When the corpse was buried, all the blinds were put up. You had to have your lamps on.

They had to stay in black for six months, and wore black ties. Always black all the time. You never saw anybody without they had black on when they went out.

Another occasion remembered by many was Christmas time. Gladys Withers (b.1900), a farmer's daughter from Babcary, recalled clearly the preparations for Christmas which included family and friends visiting in the evening.

Christmas was the most wonderful fairy-tale that ever could be when I was young. There were great preparations long before Christmas; Christmas puddings being made and there was always apple in Christmas pudding. And then when Christmas Eve came, the work would had been organised that Christmas Eve, was practically free, and my father and my brothers would go out and cut ashen wood to make the faggot. And it would be very long, long strands of faggot, of ashen branches. Oh I expect they would be about eight or nine feet long, and they would be placed together and bound round with a withy stick which is very pliable and can easily be tied, and the ties would be made, oh perhaps eight or nine inches away, perhaps a foot.

And it would be placed on this open hearth which we had, a big open hearth with a huge chimney going up. You could sit in there and watch the smoke going up to the sky. This faggot would be placed on as soon as the tea was over, perhaps about six o'clock, and friends would begin to congregate. We would all sit round this fire

Mistletoe hanging from the beams at Christmas time.

Phyllis Jones in 1980.

with the cider in big jugs waiting, and every time the fire came and burst one of the ties, the bonds as we called them, the cider would be handed round. Everybody would have a drink.

And there would be all kinds of tales of olden days going on, and the children would be laughing and singing, and that would be Christmas Eve. The children would go to bed and then very late at night, the mummers would come. They were people who dressed up, oh, dressed up terribly funny and blacked their faces, and I think we children always were glad to go to bed because we were really frightened of them.

And they would come in and they would tell yarns about things that had happened during the year. There were always happenings in a village life, and they would make up tales and songs about things that had happened in the village during the past year. And of course, they would have their share of cider, and then they would go on to the next farm and so on.

And then about, oh, oh perhaps about two or three o'clock in the morning, the carol singers would come round, and they again would come in and they would have mince pies and cider or any other drink that they liked to have, cocoa or tea. It would go on all through the night 'til Christmas morning.

Phyllis Jones (b.1918) had happy memories as a child visiting her mother's parents, William and Mary Ann Rainey of Moorshard Farm, Dunwear, on Christmas Day.

Oh, Christmas was a great do! All families went home to your parents. We used to go to my mother's people on Christmas Day. There would be twenty-five of us. Grandfather was a big man with a big moustache, and he would always have a big joint of beef. Well, when he was sat behind, I can remember as a child, you could never see his head above it, and he would stand up and carve this beef.

And Grandma would never do a Christmas tree. She always done for us children in her big lounge. Up to the ceiling was a huge, big mistletoe, nearly as big as the ceiling. How they tied it up there, I don't know. And all the little presents was tied on this mistletoe, and there was dancing. We have our meal mid-day. Christmas dinner and puddings! In the puddings there was always a sixpence or a three penny bit for each child. If you didn't have one you wouldn't be lucky all the year; you had to have some silver in your Christmas pudding.

CHAPTER THREE
IN THE VILLAGES AND TOWNS

T HE CLOSE-KNIT COMMUNITY within a town, village or hamlet was an important part of people's lives. Schools, fairs, Friendly societies, inns and churches all played their part. Although the advent of two world wars brought changes, some of the organisations survived.

Going to the seaside on school and church outings was very exciting, as travel of any distance was rare, and earning pocket money by picking fruit from the hedgerows was a way to enjoy these outings more fully. Traditions connected to the passing of the seasons and the annual celebrations by other organisations highlight a self-sufficient social life.

Although life was far from easy, with long working hours and low incomes for many, these memories reveal happiness and enjoyment, when most entertainment and leisure activities were of a local nature and therefore encouraged firm friendships.

Childhood experiences
Fairs were often held annually but have decreased in the last sixty years. Many villages had a fair which gave the opportunity of meeting family and friends. Reg Garland (b.1892), of Curload, Stoke St Gregory, recalled going to the fair at a very early age.

I can remember Taunton Fair when I was a boy; there was cattle and horses up at East Reach. I was taken when a boy to Westonzoyland Fair, and my mother made a suit for me. She didn't think I had anything fit to wear. She got up early and made this suit. We had to go round and visit all the relatives after the fair was over. We used to go to one place for lunch and another for tea.
My father always sold colts at various fairs. One of our carters would take the mare and colt to Westonzoyland Fair. Say it was bought by somebody at Highbridge, he had to walk that colt down to Highbridge and then ride the mare back again. Father

Tor Fair, Glastonbury in 1908.

Michaelmas Fun Fair at Bridgwater during the day; the farmers and animals are just visible on the far side.

usually made about £20 on a suckler colt. All the selling was done privately.

Olive Stone (b.1897) lived in East Pennard. Her parents came to the village when her father was appointed coachman to the Napier family at East Pennard House and lived in one of the estate cottages let to the outdoor staff. Olive went to the village school until she was fourteen years old.

When I went to school we all got little white pinafores, and two strings tied at the back. A bib would come up with a nice frill over the shoulder, and the schoolmaster used to come along and get hold of these frills on your pinafore. You never had to go to school with a messy petticoat! My grandmother made the pinafore dresses and my hat. I had some lace-up boots.

I started in the infant room; the big room had the bigger children. The seats were up the steps; there was a row in front and then up a couple of steps, and there was a little row again, up a couple of steps and then a little row again. You thought yourself very lucky if you got up into the top row.

I had the cane at school; I was too slow finding my reading. You had to find page so-and-so and the rest seemed to find their pages and I couldn't find mine! But nothing, no excuses, helped. I had to walk out of my seat and down two steps to go to the schoolmistress and had the cane on my hand. She kept a nice little ruler and if you misbehaved, it was "Hold out your hand!" Perhaps you had one, perhaps you had two. That's the way they used to treat us at school.

East Pennard council school in 1904. Olive Stone was amongst the children pictured here.

In Compton Dundon Edith Seal (b.1908), as a child, remembered the blacksmith, the wheelwright and carpenter, a thatcher and a saddler. There was no transport and often families could not afford a bicycle so they had to walk. Many walked to and from Street, about three miles, to work in the shoe factory.

I remember someone who'd gone out to Africa from the village; he'd done very well. When he came back he gave all the schoolchildren an outing to Burnham-on-Sea and he paid for it. That was lovely. I think we were all given a shilling for pocket money which was a lot in those days, and he paid all the expenses. My little younger brother was a little bit of an imp. Mothers that wanted to go could go to keep an eye on their children. I know he was in the carriage that were going to Burnham and there was luggage racks up and he got on the seat and took hold of the edge there of the luggage rack, and the window was open and he was swinging gaily on this rack and course she had to jump up quickly and close the window!
With the shilling that we had we could easily buy a bucket and a spade and there were sandcastles that you could get your mother or father to help you. They brought up water and you could fill the moats.
At school we always had quite a 'do' for Christmas; we had a letterbox and a place to post in during the painting lessons. We all made our own Christmas cards, painting,

Church outing from Meare to Burnham; July 1921.

posted them in the school letterbox and then we had a postman and he delivered all the mail. The headmistress would read out the person who the cards were for.

I do remember when there was some doubt about who Father Christmas was and I went up to Mother and said 'Is there really a Father Christmas?' She said, 'No, there isn't but don't tell Georgie, let him believe in Father Christmas'. You could get some shiny pennies wrapped up in a piece of paper and a few sweets, little packets of sweets and perhaps a few new coppers if they could find some new ones, and perhaps a pinafore for a girl and a little jersey for the boys, would come in their Christmas stocking.

Sunday school outings were another important event in the lives of children in the early part of the twentieth century. Hilda Denman (b.1910), from North Curry, retold her recollections of trips to Burnham-on-Sea by train.

I can remember when we went on our Sunday School trips. This is from the Baptist chapel and to get to Durston we used to have to go over with horses and wagons, and 'course we cleaned all the brasses up and that was one of my jobs. My grandfather

Church outing from Butleigh, late 1920s.

Boys playing marbles outside Baltonsborough churchyard.

drove the horse and wagon over and you didn't have bales of hay in those days so you put straw on the planks of wood across, and the horses and wagon took the children over to Durston, me in amongst them.

And we went to Burnham, and we were given fourpence to buy our tea, if we didn't go and have tea where everybody else had already booked up. This was down in the Puzzle Garden where there was a maze in Burnham. And that was the only way you could get there, unless they were well off and you hired a charabanc, and they had hard tyres in those days, some of the old charabancs. I'm going back to the 1920s.

Lord St Audries of Fairfield House, Stogursey, visited the local school regularly and took a keen interest in all the pupils. Lionel Wilcox (b.1919) and Daphne Cavill (b.1917), brother and sister, recalled school days and his influence.

We used to have school events. When the daffodils were out Lord St Audries allowed the children to march up to Fairfield, a class at a time. He would take us all round and show us the daffodils in the orchards and the woods. You could pick five daffodils each. We used to look forward to that.

At Christmas, Lord St Audries used to have a great big Christmas tree in the hall inside the house and he gave us a little party and everybody came away with a Christmas present.

There was another gentleman; he used to live at Stolford. His name was Colin Mackenzie, and every Christmas he used to send a crate of oranges; one of them and a bar of Fry's chocolate for every child in the school. We thought that was wonderful! As a rule we had a bar of chocolate between us. We had to share it.

Eva Palmer (b.1916) was born in Kingston St Mary, and moved to Broomfield when she was eight years old. Her father was a farm worker who regularly moved cottage when he changed farms. He showed her how to find and harvest food from the fields and hedgerows. When she left school Eva went to work as a housemaid and when she and Geoff married they lived at the First and Last pub in Nether Stowey with her parents-in-law.

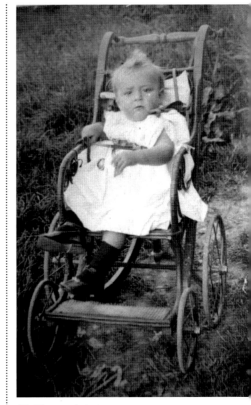

Child in pushchair.

I remember walking with mother from East Lydeard to Broomfield and she was pushing the pram with my youngest sister and she was three. Dad had gone on with the furniture in a wagon with my brothers and sisters. She was pushing the pram and I had to walk with her, and she had the alarm clock in the pram and the lamp glass so it wouldn't get broken. My Dad never went to see — he was a farm worker — he never went to see the cottage. And when we got there, which was I think five or six miles from Lydeard to Broomfield, we had to go up a lane; it was a bridge over a stream. There was a little old man living in the cottage and he came out and put an extra piece of wood because the pram wouldn't go over the stream.

Then we walked all up this lane. It was Michaelmas — September — and Michaelmas daisies out all up there. My brother had gone on before with the wagon with me Dad and the furniture. When we got up there the cottage was surrounded in stinging nettles about this high — nobody had lived in them for years! — and Mum, she sat down and cried. Me brother went out and picked some Michaelmas daisies and dandelions and he put them in an old Tate and Lyle syrup tin to try and brighten it up a bit, I suppose.

I can remember picking acorns. We used to take them to the mill down at Kingston; fourpence a pound we used to get. They'd grind them down for meal. We used to pick blackberries and mushrooms, all round the fields. We didn't pull the mushrooms, used to cut them off. Dad used to say because they wouldn't come out another year. Used to pick blackberries — get a ha'penny a pound for picking blackberries. My dad used to grow everything, cabbages and stuff and keep a pig, fowls and ducks in the paddock. We didn't have to buy anything. We used to have a man come to kill the pig. My sister used to go in the coal house, put her fingers in her ears when they killed the pig; it made such a noise to hear the pig screaming and she used to be terrified.

Grace Parish (b.1919), from Pawlett, recounted the blackberry holiday, when the school closed for the first two weeks in September.

We used to pick blackberries for our pocket money to go to the fair because in September there was the big Bridgwater fair and the children all had a holiday in those days, the three days of the fair. So we always picked blackberries and in every village was someone who would buy the blackberries and take them to market, up in Bristol. I suppose the factories used to buy them. But we always took them to a person called Mr Hagget who lived up in the village. We always preferred him to measure our blackberries because if it was his wife, if it wasn't quite the pound or two pounds or three pounds she would dock us but he would always give us the benefit of the doubt. He said 'Well, me dear, we will call that a couple of pounds, here's tuppence', and it was a penny a pound we used to have.

We used to get enough pocket money to go to the fair. I suppose if we hadn't picked any blackberries we would have been taken to the fair and given some money, but it was a tradition. I can remember my father telling me, every generation thinks that

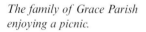

The family of Grace Parish enjoying a picnic.

they worked harder or did something different to this generation. My father used to tell me, 'I used to pick blackberries for a ha'penny a pound, you children don't know anything about it because I was only paid a ha'penny'. I suppose that ha'penny went just as far as our penny.

A family picking whortleberries in the Quantocks c.1910.

Harvest from fields, hedgerows and sea

Geoffrey Palmer (b.1915) grew up in Nether Stowey where his parents ran the First and Last public house. When Geoffrey left the local school he became a butcher's apprentice with Bartlett's, one of the local butchers in the village. His grandfather Thomas Palmer was a rag and bone man.

Picking whortleberries in the summer! That's where they made their money to get clothes and shoes. Grandfather used to buy them from the people, so much a quart. I've got the mug, what he used to measure the whortleberries, that's a one and a half pound quart. He used to pack them in little chip baskets, take them to Bridgwater Station and send them to London.

Grandfather was a general dealer in rags and rabbit skins, a little short man with a beard. He used to have a pony and cart and sell crockery, put straw in the bottom and travel the countryside, just around the area, not far afield

William Say, aged 18, in 1925.

The Squire of Butleigh, Robert Neville Grenville, a strict Anglican landlord, was seen about the village regularly, visiting the school on a weekly basis, so all the children knew him. The girls had to curtsey and the boys bow if they met him along any of the roads. Local families knew that poaching was regarded as an evil pursuit and had to be stamped out; if anyone was caught poaching pheasants they could lose their job and the tenancy of their cottage. William Say (b.1907) grew up with his grandparents in the village.

> A pheasant would often lie in the rough grass in preference to a tree. You could tell where they'd be with their droppings all around. To get them you'd lay a trail of Indian corn maize and at the end of the trail you would put down some raisins, with one raisin on a fish hook. You'd fasten the fish hook on a piece of string and drive a peg into the ground. The pheasant would follow the corn, come to the raisins, gobble them up, and eventually get the fish hook.
>
> Another way was to lay a trail of corn, and then dig a hole say the depth of a teacup and put some corn in there. On top of the hole you'd put a rabbit wire. The pheasants would stick their heads down it and as they came back up the wire would get 'em round the neck. That was another cheap meal!

William told a story about a local village poacher who was caught poaching on land owned by the Squire; Robert Neville Grenville was looking out of one of the windows of Butleigh Court.

A group of beaters having a lunch break at Keeper's Cottage, Butleigh, in the 1920s.

Rooky Nutt was a real old poacher and he was at the pinetum which could easily be picked up from The Court. Robert Neville Grenville had very good binoculars and spotted Rooky and two of his cronies rabbiting, so he cuts across the park and tackled them and said, 'What are you doing on my land? I shall summons you. You'll appear in Glastonbury. You'll hear more about this.' So Rooky said, 'How did it come to be thy land?' 'Oh', said Robert Neville Grenville, 'My forefathers fought for it.' So Rooky said, 'Well, whip your bloody coat off, boss, and fight me for it.' He certainly would have been prosecuted and fined half a crown or something like that!

As a young man Mervyn Payne (b.1926) from Burton, Stogursey, was told by elderly aunts of food being gathered from the seashore. The seaweed was collected to make lava bread and

Conger eel fishing on Kilve shore, date unknown. Group with whippy sticks.

also made into a pickle. Mervyn with his father and brother went rabbit snaring as well as conger eel catching.

> At Shurton Bars, they used to go out eeling; a couple of chaps used to do conger eeling. At Kilve they called it glatting, but I wasn't ever familiar with that name as a child. Here it was always 'going out eeling'.
> On high spring tides in September, that's when the low tide uncovers more of the rocks, and you go right out to the water's edge about half an hour or so before low tide, and you would poke under the rocks with a long nut stick, something long and flippy. And hopefully if there is an eel in there it will come out, and then they knock them over the head with a stick. And they also used sticks, road sticks for lifting rocks. I went out a few times as a small child. And I have seen a photograph of one that was caught out here; a chap's holding it up and it's six foot something. Oh, yes! That was sort of a record! They could be three or four pounds; you'd get them this size. And then there were silver eels they are smaller ones.
> George Payne was one of the last ones that was keen on going out, and two or three others would usually go with him.

Local travel

In Butleigh, close to the cottage where Christine Govier (b.1914) lived most of her life, was a triangle where three roads met. On this ground stones were brought from the quarries to be cracked for repairing the roads. Her father worked on the Neville Grenville estate as a carter. This was a time when transport for many families was non-existent, so to go to Glastonbury, the nearest town, they had to walk, go on Jim Baulch's daily wagon or hire a trap. Some local traders had their own transport, including the baker Charles Classey.

> When we were kids the quarry stones were brought to the triangle and John Charlton used to lay those stones flat, one on top of the other, making it in a triangle about two foot high, just as if it was a dry wall. He used to sit there and crack them with a hammer for the road. He were there for weeks.
> In those days Sophia, mother's sister, lived with us for a long while when she were ill, and she used to have to attend a clinic in Glastonbury for T.B. So Mother used to hire Fred Little's pony and trap, that's the way people went to Street or Glastonbury, hire the trap for three and sixpence, and take her into the clinic. My father and mother had some relations out at Pennard and sometimes they would go for the day for the Sunday, always hired Fred Little's pony and trap.

Four young ladies enjoying a ride in a horse and trap.

Roadmen outside New House Farm, Horton in the 1930s.

Opposite page: Youth club, known as the Vimto Boys after the soft drink they drank in place of alcohol, run by Canon and the Rev. Gresley in Butleigh c.1930.

Classey, when he lived down there, he had a very old car that were nearly like a minibus really, with a cloth hood. He did a bit of hiring; I remember he took my mother and father to Bristol once when my mother had to go up to the hospital.

Youth organisations

Fraser Marsh (b.1912) attended school in Glastonbury before moving to the grammar school in Street. As young adults many of them joined a cycling club. The club had been going for many years as in 1899 Fraser's father and others had cycled to see the Fleet Review in Portsmouth and watch the fireworks.

At weekends, Sundays mostly, we used to go cycling. There was a mixed bunch, about fifty-fifty, they came from the villages around. They all met up in Glastonbury and used to cycle to Clevedon or Weymouth or Burnham. We had a jolly good time wherever we went with the 'Wheelers'. We only had one competition a year as I can recall. We used to have to ride 100 miles in less than eight hours for our higher grade badge, and I can still produce mine!

If the weather was fine, we'll have a long run and go to Weymouth, or if the weather wasn't too good for us, we'd just go to Wells, or run around over by Shepton or something. We always used to ride in pairs and there was usually a

Cyclists at the Queen's Arms, Wraxall, near Shepton Mallet.

bunch of ten, five twos and then a gap to let transport pass, and you always had somebody riding tail-end Charlie, with a lusty pair of lungs. When a car was coming up behind they used to yell 'car up!' and everybody used to pull in tight and let the car pass. Oh, it was quite a thing on Sunday, the Wheelers.

Belonging to a youth organisation was an important part of life for Ken Ford (b.1915) who grew up in Butleigh, one of four brothers. Their father was a farm worker at Bridge Farm. Ken attended the local school until he was fourteen when he started working for Butleigh Co-operative Society, progressing to become a roundsman, taking groceries to houses in the surrounding villages. Later he moved to Street Co-operative Society.

> The Vimto Boys was a youth club with a captain and vice-captain. Me brother was captain, Arthur Ford, and Bert Davis was the vice-captain. They arranged games for us all and bell-ringing, skittling, whist drives, backgammon, anything that could be termed as games. We did several board games in the Gresley's lounge. You joined after leaving school from fourteen to sixteen. It was only boys and we were only supposed to drink Vimto. That's how the boys got the name. We went to the Rose and Portcullis to play skittles, but that was round the back.

Eric Cox (b.1923), the son of a market gardener, recalled social life in Glastonbury when he was young. There were many activities suitable for an active youngster which prepared them for adulthood. Eric was in the Air Force during World War II and returned to Glastonbury when he was de-mobbed.

> When I was growing up one of the big things was the Boys' Brigade, affiliated to the Congregational chapel. I was a Staff Sergeant; I was only fourteen or fifteen. We had a real good bugle band in the Glastonbury Boys' Brigade. When war broke out and the Dunkirk soldiers came back to Glastonbury, they had a Royal Artillery Regiment here, and they used our band to take the soldiers to church every Sunday morning; six hundred soldiers marching to church with a colonel in charge of them, and the Boys' Brigade Band always headed their parade. The colonel was very interested in the Boys' Brigade and every time we played them to church he gave us a fiver. Well, that fiver would buy another bugle! The band was used for all the parades in Glastonbury: the Scouts, the Guides and the Air Training Corps. The company was sixty strong here in Glastonbury. They had uniforms and they were proud of it too.

Village entertainment

Glastonbury Boys' Brigade at the Vicarage.

Joan Claydon (b.1932) lived at South Farm, Lympsham, where her father ran a mixed livestock and arable farm. She listened to her mother telling her about the social life associated with the church before World War II, and the self-made entertainment within families.

In the war, there wasn't a great deal of social life during my childhood, but during my parents' life there was quite a good one. They had a choir, most of it probably centred on the church or the Manor Hall, and there was a choral society, the Primrose League, the Church of England Men's Society, a Girls' Friendly Society and the Band of Hope. Most of these were temperance societies of one sort or another.

There was also quite a good social life around between the various farms. And at Christmas they used to go from farm to farm for a social evening, and there were concerts in the Manor Hall. My mother played the piano and my father sang, so they used to make their own entertainment.

Baltonsborough Mothers' Union on the Vicarage lawn c.1930.

Terry Knox in 2009.

Man with shotgun and his dog, used for flushing out and retrieving game.

Terry Knox (b.1950) lives in Stogursey where he was brought up on a farm. He and his brother are both tenants on the Fairfield Estate. Terry mainly rears beef cattle and is very keen on encouraging wild life. For relaxation Terry plays skittles and goes rough shooting; walking the land with a gun.

I was fortunate that I had some good male friends that we all decided to start a skittle team and every pub had a skittle alley. Eight or ten of us would drive off somewhere and meet a bunch of chaps with similar backgrounds and have a good evening and the result was immaterial. We're still doing that forty years later, but there's certainly not many youngsters coming along, and about half the pubs have now developed skittle alleys into restaurants and self-contained letting flats.

In recent years I've joined a local shoot. I always liked a little bit of rough shooting and this is a bit more organised. But we're on a 3000 acre estate here, so we rear about 2000 birds which are put in the woods in August and they become fattened up and acclimatised. The sport begins in November until the end of the season in January when they're flushed from the woods and driven over the guns in traditional manner and that takes up ten days through the winter. It is quite a social event; not large money like some of the shoots, not done for profit. The finances have just got to cover the cost.

Celebrations and customs

Wassailing in Somerset fell into two distinct practices. Some villages held their wassail celebration on the 5th January, the old Christmas Eve before the Gregorian calendar was adopted in England in 1752. Other villages held their celebrations on the eve of the old Twelfth Night, 17th January. The old Christmas Eve wassail involved going from house to house singing songs expressing good wishes for Christmas. Many homes continued another old tradition of burning an ashen faggot in the hearth, a bundle of ash sticks tied together with many withies bands. When any band burst it was time for those present to have another drink. In past times the drink was served in a wooden bowl and offered to the singers.

The other celebration was when revellers gathered in orchards to bless the fruit trees and frighten the evil spirits away in order to ensure the trees produced a good crop of apples in the coming year. There were many local variations of the wassail song, but all, at some point, included an invitation to join the festivities and enjoy a glass of cider.

Charlie Showers (b. 1906) grew up in Hambridge. His father, Frank, worked as a cowman and had sung songs for Cecil Sharp, a collector of folk songs throughout the country. When Charlie left school he worked on farms for thirty-seven years, much of that time as a ploughman. He learnt his songs from several sources, including Hambridge school and

Wassailing the apple trees at the Pike and Musket Inn, Walton, in the 1950s.

Hambridge pub, from his father, brother and brother-in-law, and the *Daily Express Song Book* from World War I. One of the songs he learnt at Hambridge school went as follows:

Through the shady country lane
Here we walk beside our wain,
Leading horses, cracking whips
Merry songs upon our lips.
Come up, steady there
Gee up, gee up, stay there.
Oh, a carter's life is a jolly life.
A carter's life for me.

Sometimes underneath the trees
We stop to eat our bread and cheese.
Sometimes at the river brink
We stop to let our horses drink.
Come up, steady there
Gee up, gee up, wow there.
Oh, a carter's life is a jolly life
A carter's life for me.

We keep our horses trim and fine
We rub them down until they shine.
The martingale so brightly shone
The little bell ring out their note.
Ting, ting, ting, ting, ting-a-ting
Ting, ting.
Oh, a carter's life is a jolly life
A carter's life for me.

In Charlie's day he and others went from house to house in Drayton on the eve of Old Christmas Day and sang songs, never knocking on a door, and if the occupants did not hear the songs the singers moved on. But if the householder opened the door when the song says, 'Pray open the door and let us all in', or something similar, the group went into the house and sang more songs and were offered a drink of pale ale. The group carried sticks and wore red and white handkerchiefs around their necks. A recording was made with Charlie Showers at the King William pub in Curry Rivel on 6th January 1984 during their Wassail evening:

Wassail, oh wassail, all over the town
The cup it is white and the ale it is brown
The cup it is made from a good old ashen tree
And so the beer of the best barley
For its our Wassail and our wassail
And I'm a jolly come to and our jolly wassail

There was an old man and he had an old cow
And how for to keep it he would not tell how
He built up a barn to keep his cow warm
For no harm boy, harm, no harm boy harm
For a cup of good liquor will do us no harm
For its our Wassail and our wassail
And I'm a jolly come to and our jolly wassail

The master and the missus were sitting by the fire
Not thinking we were travellers were trampling in the mire
Come fill up our bowl and we'll be gone from here
For it's your wassail and our wassail
And I'm a jolly come to our jolly wassail

We've not come here for to eat or to drink
But to keep up the custom and tell another year
For it's your wassail and our wassail
And I'm a jolly come to our jolly wassail

God bless missus and master and the whole family
Wishing you a happy Christmas, a bright and prosperous New Year
And many of them
Christmas, a bright and prosperous New Year and many of them

Harold Meade with a young owl.

Wassailing the apple trees was recalled by Harold Meade (b.1902) who ran the Old Kings Head in Athelney and who had worked in the cider business all his life. In his younger days cider was given to farm workers in lieu of extra wages. The daily ration was half a gallon unless it was harvest time, then it was a gallon. The men chose to carry the cider in wooden firkins. They didn't like stone jars because a stone jar needed only a slight tap and it would break.

There was the Wassail Night, what we called Old Christmas Night. What we used to do was to always have cider in a bucket, a wooden bucket. And they'd come in and dip their cups and drink a cup of cider. And they always had a given man for going up the tree. We had one of our old customers, Old Dicky, he always reckoned to go up the tree with a toast, and he sat in the tree while we sang the song. Then we didn't sing it once, we goes five or six times, and didn't go home 'til we had a belly full of cider, naturally!

We always used to put some toast up for the robin, and hope that the tree would bear, you know, heavy, next year.

There was always a belief, in my young days, that on this certain day in January, I think was Old Christmas Day, the sun shone, we shouldn't get any apples. Right or wrong? I don't know!

When we don't see any apples when the blossoms gone, they always say they've gone sheep-shearing.

Jack Richards and boy with tea for the harvest team at Middle Ivythorn Farm, Walton, 1950s.

Some of the customs that took place in a farming family were explained by Phyllis Jones (b.1918) whose family ran Hales Farm, Burrowbridge, a mixed farm which included milking cows, making cheese and butter, and scalding cream. The family attended the weekly Wednesday market in Bridgwater, where her father bought and sold livestock and her mother sold the butter and cream and bought groceries and material to make clothes.

East Brent Harvest Home procession in the 1960s.

> After they'd finished harvest, the men from the local village would come in for their firkin of cider, and we always had to give them supper of bread and cheese and pickles, 'twas generally pickled onions and pickled cabbage. You never seen lettuce and tomatoes, not in those days. Or else they would have bread and cheese and you'd cook a huge, big pot of boiled potatoes and they'd have that with butter on. Every night, oh, yes, you'd cook that and you'd be having that about eleven or twelve o'clock at night by the time they'd finished and let their horses out.
> And then there was always the Michaelmas Goose Supper for the men. We'd cook two or three geese, and they'd come down in the old kitchen with forms; there was never no chairs, it was wooden forms. And they'd be sat all there, and we would have to carry cider to them from the cider house. We would cook these geese. Mother and Dad used to carve it and put it on their plates, and used to put heaps of potatoes, they used to live on potatoes. Afters was always a figgy dough, suety pudding. They'd stay there until about one o'clock and they'd start singing and dancing.

Cecily Poole (b.1905) lived in East Brent after her marriage in 1929. She talked about the East Brent Harvest Home, an annual event held on a Thursday, in August. That event still continues, commencing with a church service followed by the procession of ninety Christmas puddings, a 120lb Cheddar cheese and a 6 foot by 2 foot harvest loaf.

> We have the pudding procession: the ladies of the village carry the puddings from the hall down to the market. Archdeacon Denison started the Harvest Home, where there were big kitchens with huge big coppers, where they made and boiled about 100 puddings for the festival. An old lady made the puddings, but when she died the recipe went with her. Nobody seemed to know what was in the puddings. Then they have carried on the tradition, and they buy the puddings now.
> We have a band which leads the procession, and they go all round the tent and they drop off these puddings for each table. The menfolk go down to the hall afterwards and they bring back the bread and the cheese. The bread is baked by a local baker from Berrow, and the cheese is being made at Unigate and that is what we always called Cheddar Valley Dairy.

We have guest speakers like the Member of Parliament. The rector is the president and always speaks. We have a procession up to the church with a band, a church service at eleven, and a fair. The children like that, and hold races in the afternoon and a children's fancy dress. We've carried it on more or less the same as it's ever been. If it's a fine day, it's a marvellous day out.

Carnival and public houses

The West Country Carnivals date back to the Gunpowder Plot of 1605. It is believed locally, but disputed historically, that although Guy Fawkes is the most well known of the people involved, the instigator was a Jesuit priest from Nether Stowey, near Bridgwater. The towns in the south-west were predominantly Protestant and celebrated the Jesuits' failure, originally just with a bonfire. As time passed they began to process to the bonfire site with an effigy on a cart. Despite the uncertainty over the origins of the carnival, over the years the carts have grown in number and complexity, involving costumes and music. Other Somerset towns began to imitate the Bridgwater Carnival and one of these was Glastonbury where Eric Cox (b. 1923) lived with his parents, who ran a market gardening business, and recalled the Glastonbury Carnival in November as one of the highlights of the year.

Wartime carnival.

When I was a boy, there was no electric and they used to carry torches in between the procession — paraffin torches — and they used to light them; and the people who did carry those torches used to get sixpence for each torch they carried. Some would carry two and they'd have a shilling. That's how they used to light the carnival up. No street lights, only gas lights then.

And they had wagonettes, not mechanised transport. You might have some small tradesmans' vans and the biggest thing would have been a fire engine. Groups and single people did walk then, pedestrians. All dressed up, mostly local people, it was real amateurs in that day. Years ago, nearly every pub had a carnival club, and do something or the other, if 'twas only a walking group of persons.

Hundreds used to turn out to see it, mostly from the villages Meare, Butleigh and Baltonsborough; they didn't come from far away then.

Another centre of social life in most villages was the public house. Margaret Windsor (b.1919) as a young child lived in North Wootton where her father ran a pub and had a smallholding milking seven cows.

I was born in a little old-fashioned public house called the Queen's Head. It had flagstones which had to be scrubbed every day. We had a wide open fireplace with two hobs in what we called the tap room. I suppose you would call it a public bar today. On one of the hobs my mother always kept a large black iron saucepan full of boiling salted water, and every day an old man would come in with a sack over his shoulder and would proceed to put handfuls of snails in this boiling water. On the lapel of his coat he had a row of pins and he would take a pin out and when the snails were ready he would take the snails out of the saucepan and sit down and eat these snails. I used to sit there fascinated.

There was much drunkenness in those days and I have known some of the men go out drunk, fall in the ditch opposite, go to sleep and as soon as the door was open walk back in again.

But we had a little room that we used to call the snug; a little square room which had the better furniture. It had seated chairs, where the farmers, and what you would call the better class, would go in there and drink whisky. Whisky in those days came in gallon stone jars.

Reg Hector (b.1923) belonged to a family of willow growers in Stathe. When he was young the family moved to North Curry, and after leaving school he became a willow cutter working in the beds during the winter months cutting and tying willows by hand. Reg recalled how

the uncut withies in beds were sold at evening auctions in the local pubs in the autumn.

> In those days I used to go cutting withies, so we always went to the sales because the merchants who bought the withies at the sales used to try to get their cutters. And the auctioneers, as an incentive to the buyers, gave tickets according to the amount of willows you bought and if you bought a large amount of willows you got a large amount of vouchers for drink. And of course they came round to the cutters and offered vouchers for drinks and tried to get them one over the eight, if they could, to cut withies for them to try and persuade them to cut their withies instead of the next man's. That's how it was run in those days. They sold them by the half acre or acre; it was usually half acre. I should say there would be about thirty to forty people there and the drink flowed quite freely in those days because of the vouchers that was given out for drinks.

Friendly societies

Bill Redding (b.1908) lived all his life in Lime Street, Nether Stowey. His grandparents lived in the same family house, and when his grandfather died there was a big military funeral because he had been in the Crimean War. Bill joined the Nether Stowey Oddfellows in 1938, an organisation which shares a common history with the Freemasons. They pledge mutual support with money collected by subscription providing help to those members experiencing times of sickness or hardship.

> I was the secretary of the Oddfellows for a good many years. We met once every four weeks, down at the pub, the Rose and Crown. We only had a small lodge. When we closed down we thought about going over to one in Bridgwater; well that closed down. There is a lodge in Bristol and I hear from them once every three months. I was lucky; I've got a small pension.
> It was open to the ordinary people. One time we had over a hundred members; gradually it went down. We paid a couple of bob a month, I think, and a small payment when you were sick goes a little way to help. We used to go into Bridgwater and had an annual parade with a special church service, all done out in their regalia and various things.

Rose Stacey (b.1898) lived in Castle Street, Nether Stowey, with her nine sisters and two brothers. Her father was a gardener and her mother a laundress. Rose, as a ten year old, helped her father rip bark from the trees on the hills for the tannery trade in Porlock. Rose

Opposite page: *Warming cider by the fire at the Hare and Hounds, Compton Dundon, at Christmas in the 1930s.*

Reg Hector holding a bundle of 3 foot buff withies.

Glastonbury Ancient Order of Buffaloes c.1924 outside the Town Hall.

Nether Stowey Women's Friendly Society annual procession to church during the 1960s.

was a member of the Nether Stowey Women's Friendly Society for many years, which held an annual event.

Most women joined the Women's Friendly Society. We had seventy to eighty members. It used to be kept up with donations, so much a year. If you were ill and in bed you used to have three shillings and six pence a week, but if you got up you had one shilling and nine pence but you didn't have to do any work when you got up. They used to wash up a cup and saucer, I daresay, and that was all. When I was a steward, you used to have to walk up once a fortnight and pay her the money, and see if she was in bed or if she was downstairs. Oh yes, rules and regulations in those days! You always had to attend a funeral, and you had to attend with a wreath.

The procession started from the clock in the Cross. It was always the Saturday before mid-summer day, about the 23rd June. The band goes in front, then eight little girls dressed in white carried baskets of flowers, then the ladies — the toffs — used to walk next to them and then the president and all the ones you used to invite to tea, then the members behind that. We used to parade into church and into a service at half past three, come out, parade all round the village and back to the Rose and Crown for tea.

Wartime

Gladys Deacon (b.1910) came to Somerset with her husband when he was appointed Chief Education Officer. Gladys joined the Women's Institute in 1939 and became involved in improving conditions in Milverton. She rose rapidly to become a member of the National Executive of the WI during the War and also held nearly all the important posts including chairman of the Somerset county branch.

When we came to Milverton over fifty years ago we, and the doctor's house, were the only houses in North Street that had electricity.

The Women's Institute were in the forefront to try and get mains water and electricity for our villages, also a good bus and train service, and police service. The Institute members were in the forefront of knitting people together; there was a wonderful spirit in the villages. And the Women's Institutes without a doubt were instrumental in helping to foster the spirit of co-operation.

During the War we had 'make do and mend classes', where we used to get sacks from the farms and dye them and make them up into all sorts of garments for the

Phyllis Jones with two evacuees.

children, the evacuees. They came in their best dresses, most of them, that's all they had — and their favourite toy, and their gas mask and their identity card — but of course they very rarely had wellington boots or mackintoshes.

The Canadian government gave Somerset some canning machines and six of our members went to a canning school, so to speak, to learn how to can fruit. The government gave us a certain amount of sugar, and one year the village here made a ton of jam from surplus fruit from the various gardens!

The W.I. ran a pig club. We were allowed to have two pigs, and we were told by the Government what we could feed them on and we couldn't give them rotten anything, it had to be the best sort of food. People used to come and bring their potato peelings or whatever. And the children, evacuees, loved this because of course when they came many of them thought that potatoes grew on trees, like apples.

Gladys Deacon addressing the Women's Institute Annual General Meeting at the Royal Albert Hall c.1945.

As a ten year old evacuee in 1939, Norman Hanson came to Butleigh with some of the pupils from Merton Court School, Sidcup, Kent. Norman has no memories of doing school work, just the wonderful times of working voluntarily on Holmans Farm with his friend, Johnnie.

Oh, the memories of Butleigh, sunny days, hay-making! We used to go and collect two large horses up in the top field. We would go up with just a halter and pick up these two horses and ride them back. You'd have to stand on the gate to be able to get on their backs! They knew where they were going; they would go into the stables and be harnessed up for the day's work. I do remember once we were coming off the field with a load of hay; we were on the top of the cart, and there was a slippage and the whole hay shot off the back!
We used to go down to the field in the milk cart which had two wheels, and a cob. Not that we milked many cows, but we did do some milking. And also on one or two occasions it was pouring with rain and we used to sit there with a sack across your shoulders whilst you were doing the milking. Yes, it was an interesting time.

Norman Hanson with Mr and Mrs Foot of Holman's Farm, Butleigh, with whom he was billeted as an evacuee.

Church and village life

Stogursey was a busy village when Peggy Elenor (b.1927) arrived to begin teaching at the school in 1964. There was a sudden influx of children from the families who moved to the village to build Hinkley Point nuclear power station and many of the families lived in caravans because there were not sufficient houses available. Peggy remembered Stogursey as an active community.

We used to have two grocers' shops, a petrol station, a paper shop which sold papers. We've lost some of those: we've lost the top shop, which was a wonderful old shop run by a woman called Mrs Glover. She kept everything, which of course they did in those days, from a pair of very large bloomers to red candles for Christmas. She had wonderful little drawers and things, and she used to say, 'Well, I haven't got 'ee but I'll send Tom', which was her husband, 'into Bridgwater this morning, and it'll be back by tea-time'. It was an absolutely personal service, they stocked everything. Of course, people go into Bridgwater to shop which is very different.
The Women's Institute, which we started and flourished, was good because it brought a big social life to the village. And, of course, some very talented people. We had some good musicians here.

Norman Hanson (on the right) and his friend Johnnie Waters in the garden of the old Butleigh Vicarage where they were billeted temporarily as evacuees.

High Street, Stogursey.

We've just joined what's called Quantock Coast Benefice, so our vicar now has nine churches: Holford, and Stolford, Kilve, East and West Quantoxhead, Dodington, Stringston, Fiddington and Stogursey. He has three qualified non-stipendiary helpers and four lay readers. I play the organ for so many of them. This last two years there's been a dropping off in congregations; we're not getting the young generation. They had a flourishing Sunday school but that's closed.

The Rev. J. G. Derrick, a contemporary of Nancy Wallis's father, wearing typical clergy clothing of the time.

The village church played an important part in the lives of many people, not just for the religious services, but also for the pastoral role the incumbent played and the social life which it generated. Nancy Wallis (b.1903) was the daughter of a country parson and she recalled that children left school at an early age, so her parents held a night school at the Rectory in Fitzhead for young men in the village where they were taught reading, writing, arithmetic and scale drawing.

Her father always wore black with a dog collar, and a shepherd's hat which was a flat crown and a wide-ish brim, which turned up rather like wings. When he gardened he'd wear knickerbockers.

Sunday services in church were well attended. The farmers and their families came in the morning and the villagers in the evening. There was superstition in the countryside. A belief was that the cattle in their stalls would kneel down and worship at Midnight on Christmas Eve. The cowman told how his father had seen this happen.

It was common knowledge that witches could change into hares on occasions. There was a hare in the district which the harriers could never kill. On one occasion some men working in the fields startled this hare and one of them aimed a blow hitting it on the leg. The hare escaped but it was said that an old widow walked lame for some weeks afterwards!

REFLECTIONS BY ANN HEELEY

I THINK MANY PEOPLE have enjoyed recalling their respective ways of life. It has been a great joy to meet and record such a wide variety of people. In a number of instances I have been able to return to the same family, often on the same farm, and record the next generation at work; this has been particularly interesting when the range of activities has developed to meet the needs of today.

I plan to continue to build this fabric of recordings for the benefit of all those who are interested. No doubt change will be both expected and unexpected and will result in a further fascinating set of recordings. For me, it has been a wonderful learning process hearing about so many different ways of life.

Sewing the cheese cloth on to a cheddar cheese at a farm in Rimpton.

Ann Heeley interviewing Ron and Ern How, wheelwrights at Brompton Regis in 1987.

ACKNOWLEDGEMENTS

WE ARE VERY PLEASED to acknowledge and thank those who have helped to make this book possible, including the financial support of the Friends of the Rural Life Museum and Halsgrove. We would like to thank all the Somerset people who kindly agreed to be interviewed: their patience, understanding and humour in sharing their memories was truly remarkable. We are much indebted to them.

We particularly extend our thanks to the following who have given us permission to use the extracts within the publication from the Oral Archive Collection at the Somerset Rural Life Museum: Pat Adlam, Geoffrey Axford, Richard Barber, Andrew Barnstable, Sally Bassford, Valerie Board, Bertie Bond, Margaret Brown, Virginia Bryant, Janet Burge, Stephen Cave, Daphne Cavill, Robert Chambers, Marion Chorley, Joan Claydon, Michael Cole, Hazel Coombes, Dennis Corner, Rachel Cowling, Eric Cox, Lavinia Davis, Anthony Dowden, Adrian Dunster, Margaret Elenor, Elizabeth Elkin, Christopher Ford, Doreen Garland, Susan Gunning, Judith Gwyer, Norman Hanson, Gerald Harris, Mary Hasell, Aubrey Hill, Dennis Hill, Michael Hill, Richard House, Ernest How, Margaret Hucker, Gillian Johnson, Phyllis Jones, Dennis Keirle, Terry Knox, Dorothy Lucas, Gloria McClurg, Liz McDonnell, Pat McIlroy, Edward Male, Irene Marchant, Mary Marshall, Joyce Meade, Nancy Merchant, David Millard, Mark Nicholls, Carole Oliver, Nigel Palmer, Grace Parish, Mervyn Payne, Mary Pearce, Patricia Porter, Margaret Pullen, Sue Rawlinson, Douglas Russell, Shirley Say, Brendan Sellick, Margaret Seward, David Sheldon, Margaret Shreeve, Frank Smith, Elizabeth Sparkes, Michael Speed, David Stickland, Jenny Stock, Janet Stubbins, Margaret Stuckey, Colin Thomas, Rita Thomas, Gertrude Tidball, Ray Tincknell, Margaret Tinney, Wendy Turney, Robert Vaux, Richard Vearncombe, Esther Venn, Joy Vigar, Barbara Vowles, Winifred Vowles, Michael & Kath Ware, Lionel Wilcox, Tom Wilkins, Cyril Witcombe of Martock, Avril Withers, North Curry Society.

We also thank the copyright holders of both private and archival photographs for generously allowing us to use them:

Stanley Adams, Douglas Allen, Charlie Anning, Geoffrey Axford, Hubert Baker, Ruth Bevan, Blaise House Castle Museum, Valerie Board, Bridgwater Town Council: the Blake Museum, Bristol Evening Post, Janet Burge, Mrs Canter, Dennis Chapman, Bob Clapp, Louise Clapp, Joan Claydon, Friends of Coleridge Collection, Hazel Combes, Dennis Corner, Allen Cotton, Rachel Cowling, Lavinia Davis, Marion Diment, Hilary Dunford, Elizabeth Elkin, Arthur Frampton, Robert Hallett, Norman Hanson, Ann Heeley, Dennis Hill, Kit Houghton, Adrian Howe, Margaret Hucker, Gillian Johnson, John Lock, Muriel Lovering, Norman Manser, Frances Mapstone, Joyce Meade, Grace Parish, Bill Parsons, Pathe News, Adrian Pearse, Colin Poole, Susan Rawlings, Iris Richards, Somerset Archaeological and Natural History Society, Margaret Seward, Gordon Sims, Frank Smith, Philips Collection, Somerset Heritage Services, Jennifer Stock, Roger Stockley, Margaret Stuckey, John Thompson, Jessie Trask, Kath Ware, Derick Warren, Roger Wedlake, Wells and Mendip Museum, Sidney White, Chris Willoughby, Cyril Whitcombe of Wookey Hole.

The Oral Recordings Group of the Friends of the Somerset Rural Life Museum has been in existence for more than twenty-five years. In that time many Friends have help transcribe the recordings. At present Mary Vidal, Yvonne Penna, Kath Cowles and Jean Bevis are skilfully transcribing from the original sound, in order that paper copies are available for research students. Since the acquisition of a digital recording machine the creation of CDs has been carried out by Kerstin Mussell. Estelle Gilbert, Site Manager at the Rural Life Museum supervises the project. We thank them all for their dedication and commitment. Mary Vidal has been working with the Oral Recordings Group since 1993, and as a result, her knowledge of the Oral Archive was invaluable in the early stages of preparing this publication. We would also like to thank the following for their support and assistance: David Bromwich, David Dawson, Robert Dunning, Mary Gryspeerdt, Kate Lynch, Norma Murray, Ann Nix, and David Worthy. Thanks also to the staff of the Somerset Heritage Service, especially Estelle Gilbert, Tom Mayberry, Steve Minnitt and David Walker.

We apologise for any errors and omissions, and copyright holders of photographs we may have failed to trace.

APPENDIX OF INTERVIEWEES

Surname	Forename	Date of Birth	Date of Death	Archive Reference Number	Parish	Date of Recording	Interviewer
Axford, 73,74	John	1910	1991	A\CMQ/2/135	Butleigh	1981	Ann Heeley
Baber, 16,60	Walter	1904	1989	A\CMQ/2/109	Chewton Mendip	1981	Ann Heeley
Baker, 41	Dennis	1922	2003	A\CMQ/2/163	Westhay	1988	Ann Heeley
Bartlett, 58	William	1898	1983	A\CMQ/2/105	Shepton Montague	1981	Ann Heeley
Bassford, 59	Sally	1956		A\CMQ/2/554	Porlock	2008	Ann Heeley
Best, 67	Vivian	1919	2006	A\CMQ/2/300	Glastonbury	1995	Ann Heeley
Board, 73	Bill	1920	*	A\CMQ/2/098	North Curry	1986	North Curry Society
Bond, 31	Bertie	1927		A\CMQ/2/325	North Barrow	1999	Ann Heeley
Brown, 94	Marion	1911	*	A\CMQ/2/200	Westhay	1990	Mary Gryspeerdt
Brown, 64	Margery	1916	2005	A\CMQ/2/481	Butleigh	1993	Ann Heeley
Brown, 68	Margaret	1924		A\CMQ/2/526	Cannington	2007	Ann Heeley
Bryant, 52	Albert	1935	2009	A\CMQ/2/492	Castle Cary	2006	Ann Heeley
Cavill, 104	Daphne	1917	2010	A\CMQ/2/533	Stogursey	2007	Ann Heeley
Chambers, 20	Robert	1979		A\CMQ/2/366	Taunton	2002	Ann Heeley
Claydon, 70,115	Joan	1932		A\CMQ/2/508	Lympsham	2007	Ann Heeley
Corner, 50	Dennis	1926		A\CMQ/2/523	Porlock	2007	Ann Heeley
Cox, 114,122	Eric	1923		A\CMQ/2/301	Glastonbury	1995	Ann Heeley
Deacon, 127	Gladys	1910	2003	A\CMQ/2/247	Milverton	1993	Ann Heeley
Denman, 73, 103	Hilda	1916	2006	A\CMQ/2/099	North Curry	1986	North Curry Society
Derrick, 39	Reg	1914	*	A\CMQ/2/172	West Hatch	1989	R Drinkell
Dunster, 48	Adrian	1963		A\CMQ/2/155	Compton Dundon	1988	Ann Heeley
Elenor, 129	Peggy	1924		A\CMQ/2/532	Stogursey	2007	Ann Heeley

Flatt, 95	Hugh	1917	2008	A\CMQ/2/462	Huish Champflower	2005	Ann Heeley
Ford, 114	Ken	1915	1998	A\CMQ/2/130	Butleigh	1986	Ann Heeley
Garland, 99	Reg	1892	1984	A\CMQ/2/111	Stoke St Gregory	1980	Ann Heeley
Govier, 63,110	Christine	1914	1997	A\CMQ/2/146	Butleigh	1988	Ann Heeley
Hanson, 129	Norman	1929		A\CMQ/2/475	Butleigh	2006	Ann Heeley
Harris, 67,78	Joyce	1919	2006	A\CMQ/2/079	Congresbury	1987	Ann Heeley
Hasell, 28	Maurice	1918	2009	A\CMQ/2/127	Bishops Sutton	1985	Ann Heeley
Hector, 123,125	Reg	1932	2009	A\CMQ/2/354	North Curry	2002	Kate Lynch
Hill, 32	Froude	1899	1992	A\CMQ/2/118	Fiddington	1980	Ann Heeley
Hill, 47	Clifford	1904	1996	A\CMQ/2/196	North Newton	1990	Ann Heeley
Hill, 19	Aubrey	1935		A\CMQ/2/358	Bridgwater	2001	Kate Lynch & John Irving
How, 55,57	Ron	1912	2000	A\CMQ/2/085	Brompton Regis	1988	Ann Heeley
How, 55	Ern	1916		A\CMQ/2/085	Brompton Regis	1988	Ann Heeley
Hucker, 13	Ernest	1911	2000	A\CMQ/2/126	Chew Stoke	1985	Ann Heeley
Hunt, 55-7	Lionel	1900	1981	A\CMQ/2/009B	West Pennard	1976	Jenny Patrick
Jones, 34	Ernest	1908	2004	A\CMQ/2/113	North Petherton	1980	Ann Heeley
Jones, 14,87,96,98 120,127	Phyllis	1918		A\CMQ/2/114	Burrowbridge	1980	Ann Heeley
Keirle, 22	Charlie	1916	2000	A\CMQ/2/075	Stathe, Burrowbridge	1987	Mary Gryspeerdt
Knox, 116	Terry	1950		A\CMQ/2/574	Stogursey	2009	Ann Heeley
Lovering, 73	Muriel	1913	2003	A\CMQ/2/071	Butleigh	1980	Ann Heeley
Male, 17	Edward	1922		A\CMQ/2/361	Kingsbury Episcopi	2001	Ann Heeley
Marchant, 65	Irene	1935		A\CMQ/2/483	Butleigh	1998	Ann Heeley
Marsh, 112	Fraser	1912	2004	A\CMQ/2/285	Glastonbury	1994	Ann Heeley
McClurg, 69	Gloria	1941		A\CMQ/2/412	Meare	2003	Ann Heeley
Meade, 119	Harold	1902	1985	A\CMQ/2/055	Athelney	1983	Philippa Legg
Merchant, 77	Tom	1914	1998	A\CMQ/2/112	Spaxton	1983	Ann Heeley
Millard, 61	David	1942		A\CMQ/2/494	Glastonbury	2006	Ann Heeley

Nicholls, 48	Mark	1965		A\CMQ/2/155	Compton Dundon	1988	Ann Heeley
Palmer, 19	William	1883	1975	A\CMQ/2/005A	Stoke St Gregory	1973	Kate Walters
Palmer, 107	Geoffrey	1916	1989	A\CMQ/2/159	Nether Stowey	1988	Mary Gryspeerdt & Ann Heeley
Palmer, 105	Eva	1918		A\CMQ/2/159	Nether Stowey	1988	Mary Gryspeerdt & Ann Heeley
Parish, 26,81,90,106	Grace	1919		A\CMQ/2/195	Berrow & Pawlett	1990	Ann Heeley
Payne, 109	Mervyn	1927		A\CMQ/2/538	Stogursey	2008	Ann Heeley
Pearce, 77	Ernest	1907	1999	A\CMQ/2/101	Fiddington	1982	Ann Heeley
Peppard, 22	Bert	1912	2007	A\CMQ/2/329	Othery	1999	Ann Heeley
Phillips, 76	Donald	1927		A\CMQ/2/156	North Curry	1988	North Curry Society
Poole, 121	Cecily	1905	1997	A\CMQ/2/262	East Brent	1993	Ann Heeley
Porter, 66	Jim	1932	2008	A\CMQ/2/483	Butleigh	1998	Ann Heeley
Redding, 29,125	Bill	1908	1998	A\CMQ/2/158	Nether Stowey	1988	Mary Gryspeerdt & Ann Heeley
Rendell, 82	Dorothy	1906	1995	A\CMQ/2/181	East Coker	1990	Hazel Coombes
Rose, 50	Cuthbert	1907	1992	A\CMQ/2/052	Wedmore	1983	Philippa Legg
Russell, 60	Fred	1896	1988	A\CMQ/2/125	Dundry	1985	Ann Heeley
Say, 80,108	William	1907	1994	A\CMQ/2/273	Butleigh	1986	Ann Heeley
Seal, 102	Edith	1908	2005	A\CMQ/2/365	Compton Dundon	2002	Ann Heeley
Sellick, 27	Brendan	1934		A\CMQ/2/384	Stolford	2002	Katy Lynch & John Irving
Sheldon, 37	David	1929		A\CMQ/2/531	Draycott	2007	Ann Heeley
Showers, 117	Charlie	1906	1985	A\CMQ/2/082	Hambridge	1983	Ann Heeley & Shirley Toulson
Shreeve, 91	Margaret	1939		A\CMQ/2/407	Glastonbury	2003	Ann Heeley
Smith, 46	Christine	1925	2003	A\CMQ/2/183	Pilton	1989	Ann Heeley
Stacey, 125	Rose	1898	*	A\CMQ/2/161	Nether Stowey	1988	Mary Gryspeerdt & Ann Heeley
Stickland, 53	David	1938		A\CMQ/2/491	Castle Cary	2006	Ann Heeley
Stone, 80,99,101	Olive	1897	1991	A\CMQ/2/185	East Pennard	1989	Ann Heeley
Stubbins, 54	Eddie	1927	2004	A\CMQ/2/429	Wells	2004	Ann Heeley
Stuckey, 12,13,25	Ken	1911	1995	A\CMQ/2/139	Kingston Seymour	1987	Ann Heeley

Symes, 44,83,88	Maurice	1896	*	A\CMQ/2/120	Coat	1980	Ann Heeley
Thomas, 35	Arnold	1912	1980	A\CMQ/2/038	Cheddar	1979	Ann Heeley
Tidball, 64	Gertie	1926		A\CMQ/2/254	Mark	1993	Ann Heeley
Tincknell, 86	Elizabeth	1904	1995	A\CMQ/2/197	Mudgley	1990	Ann Heeley
Toose, 39	George	1901	1986	A\CMQ/2/115	Brympton D'Evercy	1981	Ann Heeley
Turner, 67,92	Agnes	1909		A\CMQ/2/229	Street	1991	Ann Heeley
Vaux, 43	Sidney	1897	1982	A\CMQ/2/106	Wigborough	1982	Ann Heeley
Vearncombe, 45	Dick	1898	1993	A\CMQ/2/119	Butleigh	1980	Ann Heeley
Venn, 80,93	Esther	1922		A\CMQ/2/470	Kilton & Thurloxton	2005	Ann Heeley
Vigar, 93	Joy	1928		A\CMQ/2/516	High Ham	2007	Ann Heeley
Vowles, 86	Minnie	1905	1998	A\CMQ/2/197	Mudgley	1990	Ann Heeley
Wallis, 82	Nancy	1904	*	A\CMQ/2/008B	Fitzhead	1974	Kate Walters
Ware, 31	Tom	1925	2003	A\CMQ/2/157	Nether Stowey	1988	Mary Gryspeerdt & Ann Heeley
Whitcombe, 21	Henry	1900	1988	A\CMQ/2/084	Westhay	1986	Ann Heeley
White, 11	Sidney	1890	1988	A\CMQ/2/136	Chilthorn Domer & Ilchester	1987	Ann Heeley
Wilcox, 94,104	Lionel	1919		A\CMQ/2/533	Stogursey	2007	Ann Heeley
Wilkins, 17	Albert	1894	1992	A\CMQ/2/104	High Ham	1982	Ann Heeley
Windsor, 66,76, 80,89,123	Margaret	1919	1994	A\CMQ/2/144	North Wootton & Pilton	1988	Ann Heeley
Witcombe, 84	Joe	1899	1986	A\CMQ/2/108	Compton Dundon	1980	Ann Heeley
Withers, 91,96	Gladys	1900	2002	A\CMQ/2/065	Babcary	1983	Philippa Legg

We have in many cases been able to establish the date of death. Where this has not been possible an asterisk has been used. Where there is neither a date nor an asterisk it is believed the interviewees are still alive.

INDEX